I Remember

Indianapolis Youth Write about Their Lives

2014

INwords

I Remember:
Indianapolis Youth Write about Their Lives
2014

Edited by Mark Latta, Darolyn "Lyn" Jones, Michael Baumann, Olivia Gehrich, Rachel Johnson, and Charnell Peters

Cover art by Andrea Boucher

Published by INwords: Indianapolis, IN

ISBN: 978-0-9849501-4-0

I Remember

Indianapolis Youth Write about Their Lives
2014

Edited by
Mark Latta, Darolyn "Lyn" Jones, Michael Baumann, Olivia Gehrich,
Rachel Johnson, and Charnell Peters

INwords Publications
PO Box 30407
Indianapolis, IN 46230-0407

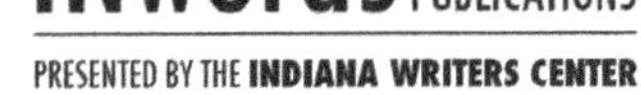

Allen Whitehill Clowes
Charitable
Foundation, Inc.

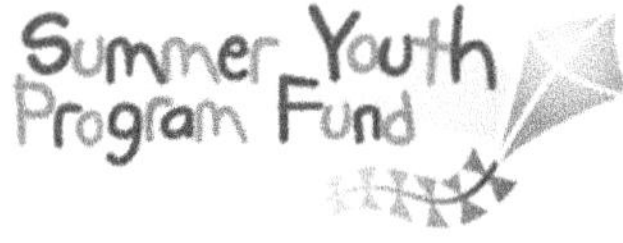

Contents

Introduction i

Writing Sites iii

Collected Writing 1

Writing Prompts 228

Cover Artist Statement 232

Acknowledgments 234

Author Index 235

Introduction

Funded by the Summer Youth Program Fund (SYPF), the Indiana Writers Center's Build a Rainbow creative writing program serves a diverse group of young people in Indianapolis, improving their writing and literacy skills through a series of creative writing exercises that teach them how to write the stories of their own lives. The program is named after a colorful, whimsical poster of a half-made rainbow that is covered with tiny stick figures painting, hammering, and operating cranes as they work to finish it. The image is a visual reminder that there are many small steps in creating something beautiful—a piece of writing, a dream, a goal, a life.

Working one-on-one, Writers Center instructors, student teachers, and volunteers help the young writers get their words on the page and also encourage them to reflect upon the experiences they've written about, considering how what they've learned can help them make their dreams come true.

Like all writers, no matter what age, no matter how experienced, the students struggle to find something to write about. "My life is so boring!" they say, frowning. We assure them that their lives are not boring at all. Everyone has hundreds of amazing stories in their heads, just waiting to come out. We talk, teasing those stories out of them. We know when we hit on the right story because their frowns melt away, their eyes light up; they smile—or even laugh.

We tell them, "Now write the story of what happened when..."

And they raise their pencils and begin.

They hunch over their papers, almost as if trying to climb into them. In that room, together, they are also at school, on the playground, at a family reunion. They're at Grandma's house, helping her cook. They're riding bikes and roller coasters, shooting baskets, dressing up their dogs in silly outfits. They're holding their baby brothers for the first time, dancing their first solo. They're eating burritos and barbecue, fried chicken, birthday cake, and Gerber peaches. They're playing hide and seek with their cousins in the backyard; arguing with their siblings, hurrying home in the rain. They're laughing so hard their stomachs hurt. They're mourning the deaths of people they love and who loved them. They're in a state of wonder watching fireworks paint the night sky.

It is a beautiful thing to watch children write, lost in those inner worlds, a delight to watch them scramble to be first in line to sit in the Author's Chair and read their lives to each other. And what a kick it is to hand out the anthology of their work at the end of our time together and watch them discover their very own stories inside!

It is a pleasure and privilege to work with the young people from St. Florian Youth Development Camp, La Plaza's Leadership Institute for Latino Youth (LILY) and the Concord Neighborhood Center Summer Program each year. Their stories reflect their exuberant spirits and offer hope for the future.

Barbara Shoup
Executive Director
Indiana Writers Center

Writing Sites

Saint Florian Youth Development Camp

Founded by Indianapolis Firefighters in 1992, the Saint Florian Center provides Indianapolis youth an opportunity to develop leadership skills, problem solving methods, and survival tactics, as well as fostering core values such as honesty, respect, responsibility, and character. After-school programs, tobacco-free programs, rites of passage programs, alcohol and violence prevention programs, college preparation programs, and youth ambassador programs are among the services the Saint Florian Center provides for young people.

The Saint Florian Center Youth Development Camp, which serves approximately 100 students each summer, age 6–18, has been in operation for twenty years. Over the course of seven weeks, students learn about the world around them and how to be successful in it by participating in a wide range of activities that include academics, science and technology, team-building, physical fitness, and art. This year, Core and Junior Cadets improved their writing skills by writing the stories of their own lives. In 2011, *Time Magazine* featured the Saint Florian Center Youth Development Camp as an extraordinary summer learning program.

La Plaza Leadership Institute for Latino Youth

La Plaza is a groundbreaking effort to be the trusted liaison between Latinos and the larger community. La Plaza exists to serve, empower, and integrate the Latino community of Central Indiana.

The Leadership Institute for Latino Youth (LILY) is a six-week summer leadership program designed to help middle and high school students gain the skills necessary to be better prepared for college, careers, and life. LILY accomplishes this goal through math and English enrichment, leadership projects, career and college exploration, physical and health education, field trips, community service, and the use of technology.

Concord Neighborhood Center

For more than 120 years, Concord Neighborhood Center has been a cornerstone of the South Side Indianapolis community. Through social services and educational, recreational, and cultural enrichment opportunities, it touches the lives of approximately 4,000 people each year. The Summer Day Camp offers students ages 5–13 an array of activities that involve education, health and fitness, art, music, and the enhancement of social skills. Its overall goal is to provide an engaging environment that accelerates achievement during the months when learning losses most frequently occur.

I Remember
Collected Writing

Andrew M.
Age 13, La Plaza

The Story of Penguins

My life all started from an egg in which it protected me during my first stage of life. I never knew what this world had in store for me. I was just a small little animal in this earth. Then all of a sudden I entered into the world. It was a world I never could of expected this. I knew I had a purpose in this world and I have to accomplish it.

The Dog That Changed My Life

When I adopted my dog I had a feeling that an adventure would happen. I knew me and this dog would be good pals. When I reached the animal shelter I had to snap out of this fantasy and go back to reality, I already had this dog in mind and his name was Blue. He was called Blue because he was a Blue nose pit bull. He was rescued from an abusive owner that just needed love and affection.

Abandoned Island

As I walked around this abandoned island and saw these tropical trees, the things I smelled were the fresh scent of coconuts in the trees. These trees were so tall it was if it was touching the sky. This abandoned island had nobody but myself. I feel like the king of this island and I own it. This island has no rules, no population, and nothing. The first thing that flows through my mind is building a house. It was like a mixture of a desert and a forest thanks to the beach. As I walked into the abyss of the forest it turns out I'm not alone. I found out that there were already people living in this island and I feel bummed out. This was a waste of time thinking I found this island and I walk away.

Allen J., Jr.

Age 13, Saint Florian

My First Football Practice

The grass was freshly cut
My shoulder pads were too big
I wasn't the fastest runner
Wanted to be a running back (but coach wanted me to play defensive end)
Everyone was very confused
My friends played for a different team
I hit my head on my sternum and had the wind knocked out of me
Everyone hated running and pushups

Stay Awake

I was at home watching television (Kevin Hart) when my older brother and his girlfriend and children were over at my house. My little brother had just gotten up from a long nap. When my younger brother wakes up he is very confused, so we decided to pull a prank. We opened the door to the garage so he could think we were just getting home. He came in the family room very confused so he could think we were resting. Desean (my older brother) said, "Good afternoon youngster." Jordan said, "Hello." I felt like he was so confused that I should say we missed camp. He was so mad at me. "Why didn't you wake me up?" He was mad and embarrassed when we told him everything. Don't be confused when you wake up 'cause anything can happen.

The New Shoes

I walk into Foot Locker with shoes on my mind. No one specific shoe but just shoes. My agenda is to find my 5 favorite shoes in the store and try all 5 on. First look at all the designs and choose my favorite. That shoe will be tried on last. Ok so second my nose will inspect the inside of my shoes. I loooooooooove the new shoe smell. The new shoe smell is the best smell in the world (to me). Third is to try on one of the shoes. Every shoe is put in the 10.5 shoe range.

Every shoe is very different in its own way. High tops, low tops, basketball, and casual shoes. LeBron, KD, Kobe, and MJ. Somoas, Chucks, Roshes and Reebok. All these different shoes and all these different shapes are so beautiful. After the trying on process, I make the biggest decision of the day. Delete 3 shoes away and keep 2. If I don't want both pairs of shoes, I make a bigger decision. One pair. The pair that will last till they dry old and pass away or till I don't want them anymore. Those shoes should also know that they will be smelled every day. Those shoes will know that they're the chosen ones.

So Embarrassed

I was in 5th grade and I was the new kid in class. I knew everyone was after me because I thought I was cool. I was coming from a private school. I had the newest shoes and I was very athletic. They didn't like me and you could tell. Bumping into me for no reason. Not picking me when they played basketball and stepping on my shoes (now that made me mad). The prank they pulled on me was so embarrassing that I was called pee boy for a week. The boys decided to pour water on my seat in class. I sat down and I felt like I accidentally peed on myself but I knew I didn't. I looked down and saw water on my chair. I was so wet that my friends called me urine man, pee boy and even bladder buster. I was so embarrassed. Live never forgetting.

Not as Easy as it is Now

My parents always tell me about how life wasn't as easy as it is now. "We didn't have anything to what y'all have now. We didn't have phones, TVs, and digital cameras. We maybe had a radio and most rich families had a television. There weren't any social media websites and instant messaging wasn't invented. We had to write letters. We rode our bikes and walked EVERYWHERE. To the market, sometimes church and even to Aunt Sally's house. Y'all have these hundred shoes while we sometimes couldn't afford Chuck Taylor's. Everyone knew everyone and we even ate dinner at each other's houses once a week. And last but not least, we were outside until the streetlights came on. Y'all texting and playing games on y'all electronics while y'all could be outside. Y'all just don't know."

Azhure S.

Age 14, Concord

Sea Shell

It reminds me of
an animal skull like
someone cut it off
And it makes me think
of an animal being
hunted. It sounds like
the screaming of the
animal dying
the color reminds me
of dried blood.

Grandmother

She is tall and skinny and she
has a Beautiful shade of
Brown skin it is the shade of
freshly carved wood I love
the story that she tell me
about my grandfather and
how she doesn't get upset
when she talks about my grandfather
My favorite story is when my
grandfather would give me
candy and I wasn't able
to have it. She taught me
to never give up on hope
and no matter what life throws
at you there is a rainbow
around every corner.

Water Park

"Kobe," My Aunt screams
as we catch up with him
he is anxious to get in the
water park he takes off to
the water then he stops
Right in front of the water
he is scared to proceed in the water
he looks back at me to see
if I will join him But by the look on my face
he knows he is on his own
he looks around at the
other kids and then he takes
a Deep Breath then he makes
his way in the water.

The Boat

it's quiet then you hear
a splash I look around and
see other people on the lake
But there is no one in the water
then I go back to the Book then
I hear another splash then
I look out again but it sound
closer this time I look under
the Boat it's my cousin so then
I gather myself to Bust a
Back flip then we play for
a good hour you can see
the people by the bank trying
to fish but we don't care
then My Auntie takes our picture
and then we get out to dry off
then we doze off on the
way back to the dock.

Dylan N.

Age 13, Concord

"Boats on the Beach" *By Vincent Van Gogh*

If I was in this painting
I would stare at the boats like
watching TV. I would step on
the boats and hear that noise of me
stepping on that plank wood. I
take a boat off of the beach and move it
into the sea. The sea looked so blue it looked
like the sky. The force of the wind makes the
sail puff. The sea has big waves like
mountains that toss me up and down.

The Certificate

When I walk around my school hall seeing
all these empty plaques, I see one, only one.
Mine. I go from non-important to important, I
stayed in Indiana for my family. I am
the man of the house to help pay the
bills. I went to college and high school
all the way back to middle school. I look
back at the plaque and see one thing.
Me.

Turtle Shell

The turtle's shell felt like
a pretzel. The turtle shell cracks
felt like a new structure every
time. The segments to the turtle shell
looked like shapes. The patterns
always repeat never change.
The shell must have felt it
has a crack for it remains as a scar.

Ahlena S.

Age 9, Saint Florian

Little Fish, Big Pond

I remember yesterday I laughed real hard and my stomach was hurting because my brother told me a silly story. The story was about a silly goldfish. The goldfish was in a big ocean. He was swimming with nowhere to go. The ocean was clean, light blue, and cold. He was a little fish in a big ocean. Then I laid down and I got back to eating.

The Zoo

This is the story of what happened when I went to the zoo.

We went to the zoo on the bus. It was a hot day. First we went to the restroom.
Next, we pet the baby shark that did not have teeth. It felt smooth.
My teacher said not to be bad. We walked in a straight line.
At the end we went home.

Feeling Better

I remember I got hurt yesterday and fell off my bike and I hurt my knee. My brother helped me get up When I fell. Then my mom gave me a Wet paper towel. Then she gave me a band-aid. At the end I felt better.

Swinging Really High

I remember going to a playground. It was fun. I played on the swings. My mom was with me. She was sitting on the bench watching me. When I swing it feels like I'm going to fall off, and I'm scared I'm going to fall off, but I've never fallen off before. I like swinging really high because it's funner. The park was green, yellow, red, purple and white. It had slides.

Basketball in the Backyard

I remember me and my brother played
basketball in the backyard yesterday.
Every day when we play basketball,
I win. The basketball is orange
and the court is small and the court
is black, white, orange and gray.
When we played basketball it was
really hot. And when I won, my
brother said, "Good job." When
I play I feel real good. I have a
small court at home and I almost
made a slam dunk. I am a
basketball player.
I want to play for
school someday
and professionally.
My favorite player
is LeBron. He makes
those shots ALL THE TIME!

Holiday World

I remember when I went to Holiday World. I went on a roller coaster. It was a scary coaster taller than the sky. I rode the coaster with Alena G. We waited for 2 hours. I was so happy to be at the front. I almost threw up! Then we ate. We went to school, we did our leadership and then we played outside and then we went home.

Alena G.

Age 9, Saint Florian

Holiday World

I remember when I had a best day ever. So it happened at Holiday World and we played ball-toss and the Raven the scary ride (ooh scary) it was so fun and we ate funnel cakes and pizza and french fries. It was good. We played in the water it was so much fun then we did the wave it was big waves. Lauren did a headstand in the water. It was cool. I loved it. I loved the ride. The bus had a movie player. We watched animals movies to princess movies and Lauren and I ate candy, chips, soda, and fruit and cookie grahams. In the gift shop I bought sunglasses for my brother Xavier and for my mom I bought a necklace and for me I bought a necklace. For my dad I bought him a ring. It was green his favorite color. I love Holiday World. I think I will go more than 1 time. I <3 Holiday World. I Love it.

Fifth Harmony Pizza

I remember when I had ate my favorite food. It is pizza. It was cheese pizza. It was Dominoes. It was good pizza. I was at the Fifth Harmony show with the Girl Scouts. I will name some of the girls in the troop Lauren H, she is in this camp too she is my best friend and Julie she is nice too. I got an autograph for a group of boys and one of them hugged me. I loved it I wanted not to let go. It was a fun show. Fifth Harmony is a group of five girls. There is a girl in the group. Her name is Lauren and Lauren H. scream, scream, scream, scream. It was funny.

My Hurting Knee

I remember when I was at Jewel and I fell on the sidewalk and my counselor Reese put her sunglasses in my hands and I carried her sunglasses to the playground and when we were on the sidewalk I fell on my knee and it was blood on my shorts so my friends helped me up and my counselor helped me to the nurse's room and I was crying so hard my face turn red like an apple. When we got inside I put a band-aid on my knee to stop the blood. It was at Jewel summer camp it was a good camp my friends names are Lauren, Karyen and Ayanna it was in the summer.

Alexis P.

Age 11, Saint Florian

Double Trouble

One day at Loving Care we were outside. I had this kickball, because I took it from my friend, because we were playing. I ran to the swing, and sat on it. My friend sat on the swing next to me. I put the ball in between my feet as I swung. Then the ball fell. My brother ran and got the ball and ran. Then he stopped.

I said, "Don't throw it, just hold it." And then he throw it. It hit the tree and bounced off of it. My friend was standing next to me trying to get the ball. It was not too far away from me. We both ran after it.

I tried to kick it, but my foot just rolled over it, and I tripped, and fell on the wood. I just kinda felt like my leg was vibrating. It wasn't bleeding, it was just all scratched up.

"Are you ok?" asked my caregiver.

I said, "Yes!" She told me to come here. She looked at it then told me to go to the restroom and put a wet paper towel on it. I slowly started bleeding. When I put the paper towel on it, it stopped.

So I just went back outside. My brother had the ball, and asked, "Do you want this?" I said, "No!" Then I just went to play basketball with my friends. When I shoot this one boy took my ball. I waited till he shoot it. Then it went over onto the swings.

Me and my friend named Kaylah went to go get it. She grabbed the chains and the metal on the seat hit me hard in my ear! I walked over to the bench and laid down. It hurt so bad I was about to cry. I didn't. I guess that day was just double trouble.

The First Time I Rode My Bike with No Training Wheels

One day when I was outside I took my bike in the garage I asked my dad to take the training wheels off my bike. My dad asked me, "Are you sure you're ready to get them off?" I said. "Yes!" (My head was telling me I was ready but my body was telling me no). So my dad took them off. When I was riding I kept falling off (and so on I can't remember the rest of that day). So one day my brother, my sister, and I went outside with my mom. Some neighborhood friends were outside. This one boy that I have never seen before was riding in our cul-de-sac, and then he had a motorcycle bike (it was a bike that looked like a motorcycle). My sis got on. When I was riding around I fell a lot, but started to get the hang of it. I turned and was riding. I was about to crash into a mailbox, but I closed my eyes, and fell beside it! OUCH!!! I hurt and I cut my leg and it was bleeding really bad! My neighbor gave me a band-aid. Then I started riding again. I stopped and got off, and look at my foot. It was bleeding a lot, but didn't hurt. I told my mom and we all had to go in and take a shower. Maybe I should have the training wheels on! It felt horrible without training wheels.

Bike Crash

One day my sister, my brother, and I were riding our bikes outside. We are only allowed to ride our bikes down past our neighbor's house to the end and we seen Michael his brother & sister. I said, "Hi Michael."

"Oh Hey Alexis," said Michael. Then I rode back to my house to tell my mom that I saw him and he lived in my neighborhood. Than we rode back and his sister said, "Michael is fast on his bike." So I challenged him in a race.

So we raced on the sidewalk because I didn't want to ride in the street because it is not safe.

So we were racing, then *KABAW*! We crashed. I fell on my knee and it was fastly starting to bleed. I look at him and all the bikes were on top of him. Luckily, he had sweet pants on.

So I hopped all the way home and in the house. Maybe we should have raced on the sidewalk.

Aylin J.

Age 15, La Plaza

I Am...

I am Aylin
My name means Bright Moon Halo
I am shy/quiet, sarcastic, naive, and reader
I wonder if my family is getting a dog for my brother
I hear sweet dance beat drops music
I see the infinity sign
I taste Skittles, fruity
I smell Wonderstruck-Perfume 7
I feel pages of my favorite book, raspy
I feel scared when I'm about to take a hard test
I feel strong when I am being myself
I hope to graduate college
I am me.

Myself in the Future

I see myself in the future as a creative person. I hope to inspire people who don't like to read and involve them more into reading. I would help them choose the thing they are most interested in reading. I will try to convince them that reading isn't boring.

I'll Get the Hang of It

My quest was my first day of High school. It was about 7:00am, I woke up, it was a Monday in August, I was REALLY nervous enough though my family told me there's nothing to worry about. To make my worry worse my house was silent. Nobody was home so I had to depend on myself and time. I rarely slept at night. I got out of my bed and changed into my long jean shorts, my neon orange "Cocoa Beach" in bold letters. I put my hair into a ponytail. I brushed my teeth and dumbly forgot to eat breakfast. I kept checking that I had all my supplies and backpack ready. I kept repeating and thinking, "You're not a middle-schooler anymore, this I.D. around your neck that says you're in 9th grade and your name. If people ask about your grade show them your I.D." I kept looking at my hand that had my time and bus number. When it was 7:55 am, I closed my door, took a deep breath. Then, I saw some familiar girls that went to school with me last year, and relief hit me. Automatically my head thought yes you're doing the right thing, the high school bus gets here before the middle school one. At my bus stop, people are chattering and beyond nervous, my thoughts overwhelming me. Then...I saw the bus 96. When the bus door slides open, I thought, "Official High Schooler." My bus left my neighborhood and I thought 'no going back now.' My bus took the highway passes 3-5 streets and Voilà the brick 2 story white cement school shows up. I'm nervous. When my bus drops me off at the drop off, everyone gets off and I'm really scared, because everyone went their own way while I was clueless where to go. I quickly followed some people that led to the second floor, knowing I had to get my Spanish II textbook. I managed to get to my locker, but when I tried once, twice, triple times I couldn't open it. I felt my blood turn cold. Then maybe the 8th or 9th time I got it open. I had so many worries: 1) was I going to get lunch with my friends and what time 2) was my locker going to open again 3) where the heck are these classes. I manage to find my 1st class and luckily my friend was in there. It was mostly the teacher discussing rules, grades, ice-breaking, how high school works. I manage to get the hang of my locker, my classes, I barely got to talk with my friends because we were in a rush. When I got on the bus that afternoon, I felt relief, I survived my first day of high school but I got homework. :-(Later my mom asked me was that bad. I replied, "No, I'll get the hang of it, I'm sure."

Amiia G.

Age 8, Saint Florian

Without Training Wheels

I remember when I got hurt. It was when I was riding my bike and I rode my bike without training wheels. I was with my dad and he was right beside me. I was riding really close to the end of the street. When my dad touched my bike it made the steering wheel turn into the rocks. Then I fell off my bike and my knee fell into the rocks. Then I had a big bloody mark on my knee. I couldn't walk so my dad called my mom. She brought my bike back to the house. When my mom saw my leg she said I needed a big band-aid or wrap. When I went to school I was scared that nobody would want to do anything with me. During recess I had to sit on the bench. When it was time for gym I could do some stuff. My knee is better now. It happened in 2013. Now I have an itchy mark. But it doesn't itch. Now I am scared to ride my bike without training wheels.

My Friend's Birthday

I remember when I laughed so hard. It was when I went to my friend Amira's birthday party. It was funny because when she jumped into the pool and her hair got so, so curly and a little bit nappy. She got lots of presents. When it was time to sing happy birthday her cake was so big. She was turning 8. Her dad smashed her face in the cake then she wiped her finger on the icing and then she licked her finger and she said, "Yum yum, pretty good."

Saddest Story

I remember when I lost someone I loved. It was my grandpa, my mom's dad. So ok here the real story. When I was 5 no wait when I was 6. I don't know how he died but when I heard my mom talking about it I ask my mom what was wrong then she said my grandpa died then I said really. Wait rewind. It's supposed to be like. My mom wasn't crying she tried not to and I didn't know that he died. And when I heard about it I was very sad. When we got to the funeral I was very sad and I'll never forget him. The end and by the way he is 105.

Sister

I remember my sister, little sister really wanted to go to Chuck E. Cheese. But my mom said she had to do cheerleading. Well she did do it but she went to our mom not that many times but I didn't go to mom at all well until it was break time and time to go home but Anyia my little sister went away more than I did. Anyia kept on asking to go to Chuck E. Cheese. Well her birthday party is going to be at Chuck E. Cheese. I told her to wait until the birthday party but her birthday is on October 25th. I hope me and my little sister will have a good time but she already went to my friend's birthday party and it was 5 weeks ago but even if she is mad I still love her. And also at the birthday party it was cool. The end.

Jacob D.

Age 13, Concord

Us

Me and my brother are twins
Caleb is creative
But when we play basketball
he always tries to beat me
But he crowds me
He plays video games and he beats me
But he can't beat me in 2K but he can in GTA
That's me and my brother
we have a secret language

On Trail

I hear
trees blowing in the
breeze. The trees
have some dead leafs
that have fallen. I look
at the pond and lily pads
were floating like small rafts. Then I
heard frogs croaking.
Then I seen a turtle
sun bathing then one
jumped in and swam away.

"Self-Portrait of Vincent Van Gogh"

The colors are darker than normal
He wanted it to be dark because he wasn't proud of his looks
He has an oddly red ear
This picture looks like it's done on cloth like a rag
He looks weird his eyes are dark too

How I Want to Be

I want to be sculpted
with solid gold. I want
to be ripped and muscled.
Only grass beneath my feet green.
I want to be placed where
I first played but not in the shade
I want to be in sun to show
how strong I am.

Andrew My Coach

My brother Drew taught
me a lot. He showed me
how to play basketball
and told me all about the
basketball players. And
he taught me other sports
He's the best brother
you can have. He always
was there when I was
practicing and showed
me how to shoot
and dribble. But now he's
grown and trying to get
a job but I will beat
him at basketball one day
so I hope he can teach
me some dribbling skills
and nice moves still even
though he is going to be
busy. I thank him a lot.

Bogart M.

Age 13, La Plaza

Mom's Lesson

My mom always says, "Don't leave your stuffs laying around because you will lose it or get it stolen." But I still do that even tho my mom tells me not to. And one day I did that when I was playing soccer I putted on a car but on the windshield. Then when I got done Playing soccer I went to go get my phone but it wasn't there and I went home and told my mom and she said, "You see what I told you hopefully next time you will listen to me."

This story is about me not leaving my stuffs around. So that's why my mom tells me thing so it won't happen. So always listen to your mother.

The Mighty Maribel is always saying, "Don't leave your stuffs laying around because you will lose it or get it stole." But the fool boy still did it even tho the Mighty Maribel tells The Fool Boy not to do it. But one day The Fool did it when The Fool Boy was playing bomb. The Fool Boy put his gold on the magic carpet. Then when The Fool Boy got done playing bomb then The Fool Boy went to go get his gold but it wasn't there and then he went home and told Mighty Maribel, and Mighty Maribel said, "You see what I told you. Hopefully next time you will listen to me."

I am…

I am Bogart
I am crazy, cool, talkative
My name means keeper of orchard...and that's what my name means: Bogart. And I like that. Why? Because I like to take care of my family because they're the First thing that matters to me in my life.

Keep on Dreaming, Hijo

The first time I kicked a soccer ball I felt like happy. *IDK TBH* I felt like I was made for soccer. Why? Because I felt that passion that a lot of people can get. But yeah, every single time I saw a soccer game, I was saying, "One day I will be like Lionel Messi." And that's when I told my parents. And my parents said, "Yes, hijo, you keep on dreaming." And they also said, "I hope you go farther than that," but only one member of my family said to me, "No, you are not going to play soccer." And I said, "Why?" And they said, "Because you suck." But then a couple of months later, I started training very hard, and I asked my teammates to help me out on what I need to practice on for me to get better at it. And I have been practicing on kicking the ball right and on the positions I was supposed to do.

I was happy. Why? Because my teammates were there for me. So then I said Ima keep on training I said to my team and my team was very happy for me. Then I saw my uncle one day and I asked him for a soccer match and he said okay then once the game was over then he said, "Wow you got better at soccer" and I said, "*IKR*" and he said, "Yes."

Camran P.

Age 11, Saint Florian

My Sister

My sister, Crystal, was always there for me. She chose to take care of me. She didn't have to take care of me. She dropped out of college to take care of me. She made sure we had somewhere to stay every night. She made sure I ate before she ate. We lived in a couple different houses. We stayed with Andrea, who had a daughter. We played with her all the time. She made the kids happy. We stayed with a girl named Neisha. She had a big TV. She bought me a turtle. I named him Johnny Rico. Mama Buder let us stay with her a little bit. Then we moved to Mama JB's when I was in kindergarten and we stayed there till I was seven. Mama JB had a daughter who had kids and the kids would always play with us. We played with their dogs, Bruce and Princess, too. Then my sister got a job at the police department. We got our own apartment. She also works part time at Warren High School and at the fireworks store in the summer. She is taking classes at college now.

My sister has black hair down to her shoulders. Her favorite shoes are Jordans. She likes to go hat shopping for baseball hats and other hats that look really cool. She likes jerseys, too. But she doesn't get them for her, she gets them for me. My sister has a kind heart.

The Time I Went to Kings Island

The first time I went to Kings Island was in 2013. Before we got there my sister said me and my brother were going to boot camp. I believed them, but I knew what my rights were. Say if they said, "I will lock you in a basement with all the other kids" I would say, "No, you can't do that because I know you can go to jail." There was no point of scaring me and my brother. But instead she took us to Kings Island. Kings Island smells like water and dirty people. The people are all going to different places, But it looks like there all going to the same place. I went on The Vortex. The Vortex was almost the only ride you can go upside down at Kings Island.

Kobe 9 Elites

My favorite pair of shoes is the Kobe 9 Elites. I do not have a pair because they do not come in my size but I know the ones I want. The bottom is rubber and light, the rest of the shoe is gray. There is a spot between the heel and toes that is open. The high top part resembles a Nike sock but it's plastic. To go with my shoes I want to get all gray outfits and only wear them on special occasions so I won't mess them. My next fav are the KDs because I like the way they look. They're this low top shoe. I like the army color Easter KDs and plus the new shoe smell smells better than chicken. The KDs feel very comfortable. If I was playing in the KDs I would win every game. If I was playing in Kobes I would lose every game.

My Brother

My little brother is the type that gets picked on. He talks really fast and sometimes he spits and he doesn't mean to but they make fun of him. It makes me sad and mad. My mom says, "You need to watch out for your brother. He can't do it. You will have to help him."

Little kids make fun of him and I can't fight them. They are too little. He spit one time in the snow and a kid stepped on it and started to come after my brother. I'm not a fighter, but a lover. But it is hard to not fight those battles. I love my brother. I don't want to fight because I don't want it to be a bad memory for him.

My brother is really unique. He sees the world differently. He always sees the positive. He doesn't get mad too often. When they make fun of him, he just lets it roll off. It's just hard because he doesn't get those life lessons that there are simple people and there's always someone bigger, stronger.

I'm not going to be there forever. I can't take care of him forever. Pray. Talk to God. Talk to family members to help. Be a positive force.

Bayleigh J.

Age 8, Saint Florian

My Brother Jeremiah

My brother Jeremiah still has a nurse. Her name is Ms. Sally. His nurse always comes before we leave. He is in a wheelchair sometimes. My brother can't talk so he points and touches us to get the toys he wants. He is 10 years old. Sometimes when he wants to move around he goes up and down the stairs. When it's his milk time he will go up the stairs. Me and Jeremiah like to go to the park together. While I am playing the nurse watches him. When it's time to go we go in her truck. We go back home for his feeding.
The end.

Easy Bake Oven

I remember I lost my Easy Bake Oven when I was like 4 or 5.
It was a birthday present.
I cooked brownie batter.
It looked a little bit of blue, purple, white.
It smelled like brownies.
When I lost it, I felt sad
but it was at our old house, but we can't go back.

The Lion King

At bedtime, my mother reads *The Lion King* to me. I almost know it by heart. When she is done I am asleep. At bedtime she reads more of *The Lion King* to me again and again. I like it because it has hundreds of lions and the king and the queen have a newborn baby. Then the king's brother didn't want to join in. His brother turned his back on him. If I was the lion and I was the queen, that would make me mad. When the baby grew up, then dad taught him everything like my parents teach me how to talk and walk. It feels like I'm getting sleepy when she reads to me. I have a lamp and I use it as a nightlight. The end.

Spaghetti

My favorite food is spaghetti and mix fruit.
I always help my dad make spaghetti.
I break the spaghetti.
After I break the spaghetti my dad does the rest.
I like meatballs and pasta.
I eat it sometimes in my room.
My brother doesn't eat spaghetti.
I like spaghetti.
My Dad and I eat it together sometimes.
It's a bit yellow and the pasta is red.
My Daddy and me don't always eat together.
Sometime I don't like the pasta and sometimes I like the pasta.

No Training Wheels

I got hurt when I was riding my bike. I was by myself. I fell off my bike and I got scratches. I had no training wheels. I was eight. I have a scar on my leg. It didn't hurt. It was summer. After I practiced riding my bike I was riding by myself with no training wheels, and that is when I fell.

Danny G.

Age 13, La Plaza

My favorite....

The moisture inside me is watery juicy. It mostly takes up my whole personality. My hard outer shell is so hard it can protect me like a shield. But don't drop me I'll go mushy inside. I am very big. I can feed a whole family. I am very special and very known in some countries. Most people eat me in the summer. I grow on vines. I have vibrant colors and a round shape. I am also very good with chile or salt but I'm best all natural. What I am called or what I call myself is "Eatable water."

My favorite fruit the watermelon is so watery and juicy that it explodes in your mouth like T.N.T. It's so big it's like an extra moon. If I were a snake I would just gobble it up. Even though that melon would be sitting there for ages, it would be an honor. Watermelons would be better with something like salt and I tried it and it tasted like candy on a party. The time I eat watermelon is when it's available. It's very heavy but that's why I get the big ones. Just more eatable water for me.

And for all good food there is also a dark side to it. Not any food can be perfect, and for watermelons the dark side can be very scary. I remembered one time that my friend gave me some watermelon but it won't any ordinary watermelon when I took my big first bite it tasted repulsive. The flavor just raced through my taste buds and I just spitted out of my mouth. It was an experience I never experienced. It tasted like garbage mixed in with sweat. It left a bad flavor in my mouth for a long time.

There's always been a good or bad thing with having to do with something you love.

The Astrologist

I've been in a lot of places in my time. I've also played the trumpet back then. It was very different the first time I'd played because that trumpet was broken. But that was some time ago. Not long after that I was invited to play a competition. The most important thing I have is my inspiration that I get from other people. My main quest will be tough and hard and long. I am still working on it. I still won't know what my conclusion could be.

I Do Want a Challenge

The time I hated doing something—it was school, the thing everybody hates.
My mentor is the internet. It teaches me everything. It made me much more interesting.
My obstacles are that if it could be too hard or I dislike interest in it. I have heard it could be a challenge, and I do want a challenge.
The hardest (toughest) thing could be is the work and dedication that I need.
I would have grown smarter much more smarter, I would be the first person to be on a new galaxy.

Turtle is Life, Turtle is Love

I am turtle. My life all started when I was in a tiny egg. It was a thing I called "home". I knew if I stayed there I knew I would be happy. For eternity, then SUDDENLY I saw the light to a new world. I was so frightened then it Cracked! Then it happened.... I saw an opened world. It was much much more bigger.

I got out of my shell and what I saw was that I can move around. I was very different and much sorter. The most saddest this is I had no shell or "home."

Chauncey A.

Age 11, Saint Florian

My Best Friend

I remember when I lost my best friend to stage 4 stomach cancer we used to always call each other funny names and laugh at each other's jokes. When my teacher told me Rily had cancer I just froze. The last time I saw her she was very skinny and had an oxygen mask on and she could not talk. A few weeks later I was having fun with my friends. My teacher told me, "Chauncey, if you didn't know, Rily died today," and it didn't really seem like she cared. I started crying and I couldn't breathe. My mom and Dad were very good at cheering me up. Still today I miss her and I know she's in a better place now.

Rily's favorite color was red she had dark red hair she was very skinny when she had cancer and she had freckles.

Marauders vs. Spartans

I remember when I scored 20 points in one game and I had 14 rebounds and I had 6 assists. I love basketball and one day I'm going to be in the NBA. My team name was the Mt. Vernon Marauders. My teammates' names were Daniel, Ben, Jack, Scott, Kade, and Nate. I had 2 and 1's to win the game. I was sweating buckets of sweat, everybody was cheering my name when I got my and-1 my teammates were jumping on me. I was so happy. The team was called the Greenfield Spartans. When we beat them they started crying. My mom and dad, Karen and Manfred, and my sister Sinclair were very supportive. I ended the game with: 20.0 PPG, 14.0 RPG, 2.0 SPG, 6.0 APG, 7.0 BPG, and 2.0 ARPG.

Girl Bully

I was on the playground. There was this girl who liked me and I didn't like her. So I was walking on the playground and Skylar AKA Dora the Explorer came up behind me and pantsed me. I was so embarrassed. This was not the only thing she did to Me. She also hit me with a granola bar in the face so after what she did to me I never talked to her again.

Chris M.

Age 10, Saint Florian

Future Comeback

In the car headed to the game we were down by 5 pts. When I got there. Coach put me in the game. My team passed me the ball and I made my first point of the game and then I kept scoring. We started to win. I kept getting fouled and I scored two. I started missing free throws and they started to win by 5 with 1 min. left. I heard my fans cheering, "Let's go, Chris! Let's go!" and then 3 pts. with 10 sec. to go. I thought it was my fault we lost. They held the ball until 10 sec. were up and we lost. I felt bad. The score was 31-28. I make myself better so when we come back we will win. It is important to know my story because you can learn from mistakes.

The Vortex

I remember when I was nine and I went to Kings Island. I got on all these roller coasters with my brother. I remember The Vortex. You start out going up this tall hill, turn, and then go up another really high hill. It stops and takes your picture and then it does four loopedity loops and then it goes up and takes a sharp turn right and then it goes straight and fast and then it stops really hard. I rode it five times. The loopedity loop was my favorite part. I didn't feel sick, and I even ate before. Roller coasters are fun because of the twists and turns and it's mysterious—it goes underground and you don't know what to expect. I like the suspense and the unexpected!

The Crescent Moon Scar

I've got a crescent moon scar on my chest right next to my right arm. So I was playing around on log seats outside in the front of the camp and I got pushed. I was lucky I did not hit my face and I hit my stomach and my chest. I fell onto the seats and got my scar. I started crying, so the counselors cleaned me up and gave me a Band-Aid. The counselors were looking for the boy who pushed me. The counselors were keeping me calm so I would stop crying. When the counselors found the boy they made him do pushups. My brother help me put on band-aids. I felt good because he was being a nice big brother. When the band-aids came off, my cut was healed.

Alyssa H.

Age 7, Saint Florian

I Fell Off My Scooter

This is the story of the time I fell off of my scooter. So once upon a time I went to my friend's house and I rode my scooter. I went to ride around the Block once, and then twice and when I went around the Block the second time that's when I fell. Oh I almost forgot the wheels on my scooter light up. But that's kind of a story for another time. So I fell and then I scraped my knee and it was Bleeding and then I cried like a little Baby. My friends asked me am I OK and I said yes. Then I went around. This is How I cried: "Ah no a a a a a a a a a a a a a a a wa wa wa wa wa wa wa wa wa wa wa snif snif snif." I was about to go home. I was so sad and my friend's dad asked me am I OK and can I ride my scooter and I said, "Yes."

Next-Door Neighbors

This is the story of the time I went to my next-door neighbors. Once upon a time I went to my next-door neighbors. I played mom and dad with Ashly and Jr. Ashly was the mom, I was the Daughter, and Jr. was the dad. We pretended like it was my birthday. So Ashly got my scooter and she pretended like it was my birthday present. So when I rode it, I saw fireworks. But that's a whole 'nother time. But anyways the wheels on my scooter light up.

Roller Coaster Ride

This is about the time I went to Disney World and rode a roller coaster for the first time. I went on this ride I forget what it was called but any way so I got on the roller coaster and I went really high and I came down and I twisted when I was coming down and then I went into a tunnel and I was in the dark and then I stopped and there were some lightning and then I saw a edge and it was fake and then I went backwards in the dark curvy wervy and then I stopped and then I saw the Abominable Snowman. I think that was his snow but any way he was ripping up the tracks and then he jumped down and I went forward. And I went twisty wisty and my mom my dad and my brothers and then it was over the end.

Darolyn "Lyn" Jones

Lead Instructor, Saint Florian

Somewhere Over the Rainbow

The colors of the rainbow so pretty in the sky
Are also on the faces of people passing by
I see friends shaking hands
Saying, "How do you do?"
They're really saying, I...I love you

I hear babies cry and I watch them grow,
They'll learn much more than we'll know
And I think to myself
What a wonderful world

The adapted Garland lyrics of Hawaiian singer Kamakawiwo'ole's song, "Somewhere Over the Rainbow" remind me first of my own hard life growing up. I must have watched *The Wizard of Oz* a hundred times and sang this song a thousand, imitating every vibrato Garland used when she sang it.

I loved this song because it was sad and hopeful—like me.

I dreamt of being swept up and out of where and how I lived so I too could find that yellow brick road to a better life. I dreamt of what was over the foothills, in the valley where pretty suburban houses lined the tree-lined roads like a delicious dish of Dippin Dots.

I was lucky. I did find my way out of Kansas and my Oz is beautiful. I have been teaching for 24 years, and I remain drawn to those sad and hopeful students who remind me of my own younger self.

And nowhere else is that pain felt more than when you teach what I refer to as "the littles" or early elementary age students. They haven't learned to filter. They don't yet know what society teaches us about not sharing or revealing too much about ourselves. You ask them a question, and they will answer it with brutal honestly.

If you ask them to remember someone or something they lost, they will immediately go to the saddest memory they have and divulge it like it's their last confession. They will tell you every sensory feeling in detail. It's genius. I wish I could bottle that ability they have and mix in the literacy skills they have yet to learn because these kids would be Pulitzer Prize winners. Once they hit age 11, they begin to experience fear with writing and they protect and bury their words and we spend a lifetime in the teaching and literary world trying to help them rediscover their 6-year-old self.

In the last four years of teaching with "the littles" at Saint Florian, I do hear those "babies cry" on paper and I do "watch them grow." They bloom in body, spirit, and in words.

Our summer youth memoir writing program is called Building a Rainbow and is based upon an image of a half-made rainbow covered with tiny stick figures painting, hammering, and operating cranes and trucks as they work to finish it. The image is an effective visual metaphor and a useful reference point for our young writers because it teaches them that there are many small steps in building anything beautiful—a dream, a piece of writing, a life.

As the director of the summer Build a Rainbow program, I remind our instructors, our interns, and our volunteers to remember that it is an honor to be trusted with someone's story, and to be respectful if students don't wish to share certain events with you.

We also teach our team that good writing should:

- Come from the heart and gut.
- Create a picture in the reader's mind.
- Create feeling in the reader through action and detail rather than through explanation.
- Reflect a sense of discovery, the feeling that there was a question behind the writing, something of importance to the writer that needed to be understood and/or an issue that needed to be resolved.

One of my "littles" this summer nailed every one of those bullet points every time she sat down to write. She struggled to physically write because she is still learning how to form letters but she would tell me her stories and I would help her write them down. As soon as I asked the writing question, she had her story, her answer and she couldn't wait to get it out of herself and onto paper. She spoke with such urgency that I could barely keep up with her. My pencil never left the page as she talked.

She wrote about how someone broke into her house and stole her movies and television and how sad and fearful she was. She wrote about how her parents choked one another, and how hard she cried because they wouldn't stop. She wrote about how much she loved her mother and how when she died, she pretended to be asleep during the funeral because she was afraid she would cry and she didn't want to say goodbye. She wrote about wearing her favorite pink shirt that has a letter "M" on the front because "The M shows that I have a mom."

Out of the mouths of babes.

Her head and eyes bob and weave trying to maintain eye contact with me while I scribe because she wants me to not only hear it, but see it, understand it, and experience it like she did. Her voice is sad but also intense when she talks, yet she always ends with a smile and a hopeful conclusion, remembering happier times like when she and her mom dressed up like half devils and half angels for Halloween and went trick or treating. Or how she still plays with a Barbie her mother gave her that has a long black ponytail. Or how special her grandmothers are who now care for her.

Someday I'll wish upon a star,
Wake up where the clouds are far behind me
Where trouble melts like lemon drops
High above the chimney top
That's where you'll find me

I hope she keeps daring to write and dream. I hope her troubles melt into the pages. I hope she finds her way over the rainbow.

Somewhere over the rainbow bluebirds fly
Birds fly over the rainbow. Why then, oh, why can't I?

You can, sweet girl, you can. Thank you for trusting me with your tales.

"Over the Rainbow," *AZLyrics*, n.d. Web, 12 July 2014.

Ayana P.

Age 13, Saint Florian

Falling in the Hallway

One thing that made me laugh yesterday was when I fell in the hallway in front of everybody at camp. I was running down the hallway to go outside and I slipped on an unpeeled orange. When I slipped I was in the splits with one leg fully extended in front and one bent up behind me. The half peeled orange rolled by the door that I was going out. Everybody including me started laughing. After about 10 seconds my friend Allen helped me up. When I got up I walked outside talking about it then I had to go inside to practice our dance. When I fell I wasn't even embarrassed I just found it very funny and shocking. THE END!

My Daddy!

People consider my daddy to be my twin and that I'm a daddy's girl. Some things me and my daddy share is our attitude because we both get irritated really easy and we both have a smart mouth. The two people that say we mostly look alike and act alike is my mommy and my big sister. We have the same smile and nose and the same personality but he never wants to admit that we do. One day my mom was talking about going to the grocery and me and my daddy started saying how she go to the store everyday to get something and still don't get everything she need. We also share a similarity because we talk about almost everybody. We say that's weird lookin' or have some crazy lookin' clothes on. Like on the 4th of July this little boy and his dad was running and the little boy looked strange running...like he gone fall or something and I think he might of had a mental problem...but me and my daddy started cracking up.

Trying to Dance

I remember when my Daddy embarrassed me when he was so-called trying to dance. We was at our family reunion and some music come on and he just started dancing. I felt so embarrassed even though it was just around my own family. I tried to get him to stop because everybody was looking at him and laughing but he wouldn't so I just gave in.

Jeffrey G.
Age 12, Concord

Colorful Rainbow Rides

I heard screaming on
the colorful rainbow rides and the
kids big, tall, skinny were there.
We ate a lot of food. I ate so much
food it felt like a holiday. The
smell attracted me and my
family like magnets. I felt like
I could eat a horse.
Roller coasters go so fast they
give you a wonderful cool breeze.
They go a million miles per hour.
Roller coasters big, small,
metal, and wood.
Rides making sounds
like *zoom*, *whoosh*, *clickety-clack*, and
zroom. Being on a roller coaster
feels like you're about to fall off.
There was food such as
hamburgers, hot dogs, ice cream, nachos,
soda, and so much more.

Cowries

Loneless shell once
occupied. Feels like new
soft marble. Spots as if
it is a cheetah gleaming
in the lights. Bottom soft
and white like snow beginning
to fall. Nothing inside
as an abandoned warehouse,
dark and plain for years
and years.

Mom

Mom is care giving because
she loves me. She give me things like
meals and gifts. She's a single parent
with 3 kids to take care of.
I don't know how she does it.
She make sure we eat before her.
Sometimes she doesn't get to eat.
She is like a bear that takes
care of her cubs.

Ashantē C.

Age 13, Saint Florian

Smelling Like Chicken

I walked in the house just coming from track practice. Guess what I smelled...Fried Chicken. I had knew my mother was cooking it, because it's a habit for her. My mom greeted me, "Hey baby, how was track?" I replied, "Good." She said, "Come eat, everybody!" My older brother ran to the kitchen and pushed me out the way. I yelled, "Excuse you!" I went out the kitchen to go wash my hands. I came back to eat my chicken. After I ate I waited 30 minutes. Then I did 25 jump and jacks, 25 sit-ups, and 25 pushups. I was so sleepy so I changed and I got my clothes out for school. I hopped in the bed. Eight hours passed. I woke up got in the shower. I went to school and everybody was like, "You smell good, Ashantē." I said, "What I smell like?" They said Chicken. I ran to the bathroom and texted my mom, "You got me smelling like chicken."

Audition

I remember when I auditioned for Anointed Expressions of Praise. I had on black leggings and a white v-neck. I introduced myself to Mrs. Taylor, "My name is Ashantē, I'm 13, I go to Belzer, and my hobbies are dance, Drill team, and band." Then I filled out my registration sheet. I was looking at the paper like what is this. Then Mrs. Taylor started explaining it. Next I had plugged my phone up to the speakers. I flipped through my phone for the song "Rain on Us" by Earnest Pugh. I finally found the song; I instantly got nervous and I started to rub my face. Then after a minute or two I started the song and I started to dance gracefully and let God use me. I finished dancing after two minutes of the song as Mrs. Taylor gave me a round of applause. Telling me I did so good. Then she said, "This is a big commitment, you have to go to bible study every week."

Taylor Frymier

Student Teacher, La Plaza and Saint Florian

Pages

Once upon a time there was a man. He wasn't sure what to make of himself, his life. For a time he was convinced that he should be a priest. But when he went to school for the ministry it turned out that "God's work" was far too rigid for him. Soon he dreamed of creating music and travelling as a minstrel. People claimed that his lute playing was exceptional and his voice was pleasant.

Eventually, however, his music didn't provide enough money to support him and his wife. After much searching he eventually set his mind on becoming a teacher. He studied hard and worked through much adversity but soon he got his first teaching job.

The students were hungry for knowledge but afraid to express themselves. They feared judgment; exposure scared them, and so they ignored the man when he asked them to write about their lives. They looked at him with blank expressions and empty eyes that told him, "You can't do this either". It was one more venture he was no good at. The man's heart sank into his stomach and he walked away from the class defeated.

One day he was sitting under a tree reading a book. He looked out across the verdant field spread before him. To his shock it was covered entirely by blank pages dressing the horizon in a crinkly snow. As he walked through the hooded meadow the pages began filling with inky script, though messy and devoid of reason. Each step caused a ripple of penning written by a thousand invisible hands and with each footfall the words began to form sentences. Then the sentences began to make sense. Then the sentences became paragraphs and the paragraphs into stories then the stories became images and the images danced in front of the man who saw, in wonder, himself, painted, with words, on the pages. He picked up the page, in which he saw himself mirrored, and a single sentence formed in flowing black script: "I remember..." He spoke the phrase aloud and as if the words were a mystical spell the pages flew into the air with a deafening whoosh. The crumpling pages soared, ruffling, into the sky like a snow the clouds wanted returned to them. The pages formed the words in the sky like an airplane painting smoke into a message and then they disintegrated, disappearing into the blue.

The man looked down, a single page in his hands, the field returned to its green standard. On the page was written a story titled "I Remember" and authored by one of his more resilient students. Reading it over he quickly folded the paper and took off, running across the lush field his heart racing with joy. He got home and wrote those magical words down on a piece of paper and began planning.

The next day the bored students sat, sagged really, in their desks, teacherless. Suddenly, like a gust of wind the doors burst open and the man marched in with stacks of blank pages in his hands. He said to the students:

"Start with what you remember." Passion blazing in his eyes. "Tell me the story of when..." and with that the students began to write. Tentatively, they recorded their memories, their lives, and their souls onto the pages. Guided by pure memory, they scribbled out their history, their words, their thoughts, wants, desires, hopes, dreams, loves, losses, the things they found beautiful and hideous, the things that inspire them and frighten them. They wrote stories of glory and pain, novels of the heart and narratives from their minds, their souls took solidarity on the page.

Soon the classroom was filled with pages containing the words of each student, powerful and immutable in presence and permanence. The students looked at their words with pride. The man then gathered up every page and told the students they could go home, that he could teach them no more, but to never stop expressing themselves through writing.

With pages in hand the man set to work picking each student's best, strongest piece and setting each aside into a neat pile. It was tedious and heartbreaking work; each word he read caused him to appreciate each student more. Eventually he found each student's masterpiece and tucked them away. His confidence was high, he had found his calling and he lived happily ever after...

... Once upon a later time the students were grown and living on their own, in their own lives and loves and jobs. Some still wrote a little and some still wrote a lot, one girl is now a published author, another two became poets. A few boys went on to be great athletes, all playing sports professionally, and one became a world champion. Two or three became teachers, like the man, teaching mathematics and history to children, one even taught children who had difficulty learning. That girl also wrote non-stop and became a published poet.

One boy became an Astrologist, a professional star-gazer, whose wonderment of the universe led him to discovering a whole new solar system. Another girl studied medicine and now heals people every day with her skill and care.

One boy, who is now a man, is a total hero, my hero. He's a father and husband who's strength and peace and wisdom cause many people, including myself, to look up to him.

Some of the students practiced for hours and hours, and even a few minutes, to perfect their skills as musicians. They were beautiful pianist, smooth saxophonists, and angelic singers. One girl became and architect and designed a whole city to the west. Another girl studied harder than anybody else and now protects those who can't themselves in the courtroom. She studied law long and hard to be able to defend the weak.

Yet another girl did everything in the world and travelled for years and found inner peace through her journey. And another girl became a dancer who moves more beautifully than art itself, she becomes art every day. One boy made games for children so that they could feel happiness all the time. That same boy, now man, speaks poetry at the local pub every night.

And finally one particularly quiet boy continued to learn, study, and grow in wisdom and intelligence. He never stopped seeking knowledge.

One day each one of the students opened their door to welcome the day and noticed a small brown book resting on their doormats. In gilded letters it read "I Remember" across the front. They each picked up the book and cracked it open, finding their names within the freshly printed pages. They read their stories, their memories, seeing the beauty and grace of their words. Their hearts filled with wonder in their own world and excitement for the future. They stepped out of their doors with confidence. The words of their hearts echoed within their souls for the rest of their lives and they also lived happily ever after.

Ashley W.

Age 9, Saint Florian

Family Story

Ashley the Model. That's a story that is very Famous in my family. Ashley the Model is a story about me when I was born. I came out posing like a model. I had one hand on my and one hand on my hip. I looked ama-zing. I still do. I don't want to be a model. My dog does. He love to play dress up. I don't. His favorite outfit is a biker and a rock star. He is so cray cray.
The End

Midnight Breakfast

My mom told me to make breakfast. I was up on the computer playing games. And we didn't have dinner. And I knew she was playing and kind of serious and she yelled, "Ashley, you up?" And I said yea. "Make me breakfast." I made pancakes, biscuits, bacon, sausage. I made me some stuff, her some stuff, and my boyfriends some stuff. 12:43 is early in the morning and I like that people say, "You are a little girl and you can't be up this late and make breakfast."

Hurt

One day when I went roller-skating I broke my ankle. I was at Roller Cave and that bump when you first step onto the skating floor I tripped when I tried to come off the skating floor. My fault I was playing tag. I came with my ex-friend David and my twin sister Aasha. We walked in the door and some of our friends from school. We all got our skates. David and his brother Dalen were playing tag first. Next we were all playing. When I tried to get away I was skating towards the bump and normally I step over but someone cut me off and I tripped. I went to the hospital and they told us it was fractured. After another test they found out it was broken.

Runway

One day at my house me and my sister Aasha were having a fashion show. *CLICK! CLICK!* went the camera. "Oh Oh Miss Ashley how do you look so wonderful," said the photographer, Aasha. I was wearing a long dress and it was blue. It was my mom's. I tripped over the dress then I got up and fell because I lost my balance in the heels. The heels are long they go to your kneecap. The photographer said she will put the pictures from when I fell in the news. I FELL A LOT. The END.

Aasha W.

Age 9, Saint Florian

The Principal

One day when I was at my old school I just did not like my principal. He was very mean. One time I threw up in the hallway then he just came running to me. When he came running toward me I guess he didn't see my accident on the hallway floor and he fell right in the throw up. He got up and said, "YUCK!! What did you eat?" He went in the bathroom and helped me up.

That Was So Fun!

One day when I was at school my class just got out of the gym then, our teacher pulled 4 girls to the side. Then, we all asked, "Am I in trouble?" Then, our teacher said no, Myles just wanted me to give you this.

"What is it?"

"He wanted to give you an invitation to his birthday party."

"Ooh!!!"

"Don't open it now, open it at home."

"Why?"

"You can't open it now because a lot of other people didn't get invited."

After that day it was Saturday that when it was Myles' birthday. That's when I woke up and I opened it. And we found the address and drove up there. But, first we made a stop at CVS and got him a present then went to Sky Zone and we had a good time!

The End. Thank you for listening!!!

I'm So Sorry

I remember when I was at camp and it was the day of the talent show. There was a lot of talent show there was dancing, singing, and African dancing. There was about 20 talents. We went through the talent show so fast it felt like it was only 3 minutes. After the talent show we got to play in the gym and that's where the talent was at. I was in a bad attitude because my twin sister Ashley kind of messed up our act of the talent show because she was singing louder than me and she couldn't sing. I was so mad I had to let out my anger but in a safe way. So I went in the bathroom and I was jumping around and then I accidentally punched someone in the eye. I said, "I'm so sorry." And punched myself so she can feel better. She said, "Stop, you scaring me." The End.

Thank You, Mom

One day my mom took me to Super Target and I got some new shoes. They are a light turquoise blue and then a neon green at the bottom and the tongue is neon green too. The shoes I am describing you do not have to wear socks with these shoes. My mom was taking my grandpa out to Applebee's for Father's Day. So before we went to go get my grandpa first, me and my twin sister Ashley and my older sister Amayah went in the store with me because the shoes I've been wearing was starting to get messed up. That's when my mom noticed so that's why I got some new shoes. After, I got my new shoes my mom dropped my older sister Amayah off at the Pacers game then me and my twin and my mom went to go get my grandpa. I put my new shoes on then thanked my mom with kisses and Hugs and said I love her! We had a great time at Applebee's. After we were done eating my Papa was really excited about tasting raspberry lemonade. Then when we went in the car when he opened his door and hit his head and laughed. His laugh sounded like a ghost was telling me something that was a very creepy laugh. We all said, "What Did They Put In that Lemonade?"

P.S. I wear them at camp everyday! It feels like I'm walking on Air!

The End

Eduardo H.

Age 16, La Plaza

My Dreams

My dreams that I want to accomplish one day are play in the FIFA World Cup, Become a professional Motorcycle Racer in the Motor GP, to meet all my Idols like, Memo Ochoa (Mexico Goalie), Neymar Jr. (Brazil soccer player) Cristiano Ronaldo (Portugal Soccer Player), Ronaldinho (ex-professional Soccer Player), I want to go to Brazil. I want to accomplish some of those dreams before I die.

I always wanted to play in the World Cup since I was a little kid. I always watch how professional soccer players played and How cool and Honored it would be to represent your country in the best sport. When I was little and well at my age, Me and friends pretend we are playing in the World Cup. If one day I get to be in the World Cup as a soccer Player it would be the best event of my life.

My idols who I already mention, I looked up to them because, Memo Ochoa is the best Goal keeper ever, I always think that I'm going to be like him when I'm the goalkeeper while we play. Neymar Jr. is one of the best players in the world, he always trick the other players to try to score a goal. Cristiano Ronaldo is another great soccer player he plays for Real Madrid he can take almost any one in the other team. He has won I think 3 balones de oro (golden balls) which means that's he the best. Ronaldinho it was one of the Best players in the world. He still alive but he retired. He used to play for Brazil in the World Cup.

My last dream is to go to Brazil. I always wanted to go there, is one of my favorite countries. It's so cool the beaches, the view, the people. Everything is cool.
Brazil awesome.

Hola

The Journey began when I was coming to US. I was 12 when I came here. I was afraid when I started school. I felt like I wasn't part of world… Like if I didn't exist in this world. I didn't have any communication, I felt alone. One day this girl came and sat by me, I was sitting alone in the cafeteria. She said, "Hola, umm my Spanish is not good, but I'm trying." "Hola," I reply and in my little English, I started talking to her. We became best friends. She taught me some English and I taught her Spanish. The days pass and I learned more and more English. The end of the school year came and I had to say bye to Stephanie, the girl who taught me English, the cute Hispanic girl.

Two years passed and my English got better. My third year in La Plaza I met this cute girl named Elizabeth she was the sweet girl. I meet her in sunny day, in June 12, 2013. We were playing soccer.

My Legacy

First time I played the guitar I played "Stand by Me" by Prince Royce it was really easy and I liked it. The hardest song I tried to play it was "Tengo tu Love" by Siete. But the First time I played soccer was when I was 6 I used to see people playing soccer on TV. And real life. First time I played soccer, kick the ball it felt awesome. It takes your anger out or it make you thing about other things. It make you disappear from this world and make you forget about things that make you sad.

I taught myself how to play soccer with my friends. I never had a coach or somebody who can teach me how to play. I played on the streets, indoor, grass, the dirt.

I got to cross people. I learned how to cross people. That's passing to someone on the field to score a goal. I don't remember the 1st time I did it, but I did it.

Last year, I got to cross a defender, four of them, to make a goal. It felt good.

Ronaldinho Gaucho, Neymar da Silva, Jr., Cristiano Ronaldo—they cross every defender that they meet. They cross defenders like... I don't know how to describe it. I'm not like them. Not even close. But I want to be.

Guitar I want as a hobby. Soccer I want as a career. I want to be a professional soccer player where I've got almost 10,000 people screaming my name. I want to be teenagers' and kids' inspiration like Ronaldinho and Neymar are to me. I want to make my family proud. Oh—and I want to score a lot of goals. And at least win the Balones de Oro, La Champions, and the World Cup.

Caleb D.

Age 13, Concord

My Dad and Me

My dad and me always have fun.
We always have fun in the sun.
We go places and play and
sometimes we stay and play. We
always have things we don't want
to do, but there's things we don't do.
We sometimes have to mow the lawn
and sometimes we are done and we
get tired and we both start to yawn.
But the next morning we go back
outside in the sun and we play
catch and then we're done and get
tired of the sun. Me and my dad
always have fun in the sun.

"Joseph Roulin" *By Vincent Van Gogh*

As I see him riding a bike
and throwing the morning news. And
seeing him in his dark blue shirt
and pants and his goldish buttons. As I see him sitting
down taking his break. And seeing
him stroke his brownish, black
beard. I see his old and wrinkled
fingers tossing paper and
him hold his wrist saying, "I'm getting
old."

Being a Good Basketball Player

I want to be remembered as a good
basketball player. Remember me being
in the NBA All-Star beating Jordan's
record. Remember me as the greatest
3pt person ever. I want to be
remembered as an NBA All-Star.

Remember me as a basketball.
Remember me as the best basketball
you ever had.

Remember me as a basketball
goal. A clean and round rim, with
a good net. And a black taped backboard.

Remember me as Jordan, a very
nice and caring person who helps
people. Remember me as Caleb.

My favorite teacher!

My favorite teacher is the best,
but sometimes she can get mad
and take a rest.
Mrs. K gets mad if I am not listening
She is sad if I don't work. She helps
with fractions. If I get in trouble
she fixes it. If people
bother me she tells them to stop.
Once I gave her a "Let It Snow"
coffee cup at Christmas.
She thanked me and used it every day.

Anyiah L.

Age 7, Saint Florian

Mrs. C

At my new school, with my new teacher Mrs. C, I was scared. She said that was okay, she won't hurt me. And I choosed her for my new teacher. The first time she taught me science, social studies, math, adding, subtracting. She made me feel good.

Shoe Carnival Contest

When me and my mom and my sister went to Shoe Carnival, we went inside. Shoe Carnival was having a contest for whoever picked a fav pair of shoes. The announcer came on the loudspeaker and announced, "Our contest is filling up," and, "Come on down and place your ticket in the box to get 100 off two pair of shoes." When we went to my age 4, 5, 6, and 7, I was trying to pick a high heeled shoes. My mom picked a different one that was purple, yellow, pink, and blue. I did not like it at all. I said no. My mom got upset and said, "I don't want to stay here. Hurry up." And I picked out a gray, purple and white pair. And we left. The end.

Smoke-Bombs

I remember when my mom got mad. She told us it was time to go outside so we went out on the trampoline. We took our shoes off. By my neighbor's house Miss Nancy, on the right side, of Miss Nancy, these boys was throwing smoke-bombs in people's yards. Then they threw one in our yard. My dad yelled at them. They ran away they threw one behind me. I was scared. Me and my sister and I was mad want it to do taekwondo on them we was very mad we keep on jumping on the trampoline. If we hear a pop or a boom we will drop down in our Emergency core. The End.

The Best Day Ever

I remember me and my sister went to the red and yellow park. When I got on the monkey bars, I made it to the sixth bar. I couldn't go to the last bar. My hands was getting sweaty I let go. I fell on my face. Me and my sister laughed out loud! Then I started to cry. I laugh-cried. My sister took me to my mom. I told my mom what happened. She laughed really loud. All of us! We was cracking up laughing. My sister and I got back to playing and when it was time to go, we was so tired from playing. We fell asleep in the car. We fell asleep at home at 3 pm. We slept through the whole night and whole morning and evening.

Olivia Gehrich

Student Teacher, La Plaza and Saint Florian

ZAP!

"I pushed down on the right side of the double-door. I did not see the PULL sign for the tears welling in my eyes. The cheap blinds rattled in disturbance as I stumbled into the office. A woman stood patiently waiting for me. The nurse must have already called her for my 'emergency session.' The anxiety attacks had become more frequent, the depression worse. The room seemed too tall—the ceiling miles away from the area rug that would hold my gaze for countless hours throughout my senior year of college. Dr. M sat in an over-stuffed blue chair in front of a bookshelf and a door that never opened. I sat on a small sofa at an angle from her and studied the seemingly useless bookshelves. Only one had actual books on it. A lot of things in that office didn't seem to live up to their potential. Mismatched doorknobs. Empty shelves. Empty folders. And me—an empty person. While my tears ceased momentarily, Dr. M said, "So tell me what's going on with you." And the floodgates opened into a fast-paced description of what came to be diagnosed as recurrent major severe depression. Depression is the heavy feeling in my brain. Depression is wanting to live the rest of my life in ratty old sweats. Depression is a super villain leveling New York City every day. Depression is soul cancer. I was a shaken soda mercilessly kept closed—unable to release the intensity within."

These thoughts weighed me down my senior year of college and remained embedded in my heart coming into this summer's session of Building a Rainbow. How could I help young student writers tell their stories if I had given up on telling mine? As is often the case in working with a bunch of quick-tongued, honest kids, they ended up helping me far more than I helped them. A series of jolts from these young, can't-sit-still, enthusiastic kiddos began my reanimation process.

The initial spark happened at La Plaza. Some of the students wrote with more focus and consideration than I put into any of my college essays. With the first half of the two hour session wrapped up, we took a short break. I watched all the students bolt to the restroom, water fountain, or cell phones, except for Aylin,

Katherine, and Marlene. They said, "Can we keep writing? We're not finished yet."

ZAP This simple moment shook my body with a thousand volts of inspiration. And I remembered one of the most valuable lessons for a writer to learn: If you're not finished telling your story, don't let anyone shut you up or shut you down.

The second boost to my energy was when the students were asked to write about a difficult decision at Saint Florian. As I scoured the room for waving hands with questions or tables that needed a bit of encouragement to put pencils to papers, I overheard one student musing about the idea for her story. "I am writing about a hard decision—I mean the type of decision that can change a life!" Dylan said with all the conviction and seriousness of an adult. The story was about deciding what kind of big sister to be to her little sister.

ZAP Dylan understood something that I had long forgotten: You have important choices in how you *react*, even if the *event* is out of your control.

A third very powerful shock to my system involved the best kind of medicine: laughter. Jeremiah K. proudly sat in the Author's Chair to share his story about something that made him laugh so hard his stomach hurt. He proceeded to recall the time when a camp counselor "farted real loud that all the windows busted. Me and the other Jeremiah cracked up... It smelled like rotten eggs that a skunk poo-pooed on." A chorus of shrill laughter burst out through the entire room, as if a wave of the same joyful emotion took over everyone in sight.

ZAP This moment revealed a couple of things. First, kids are going to be kids, which almost makes their intense moments more meaningful. Second, having a well-balanced outlook on life requires both seriousness and laughter among other emotions. Plus, everyone laughs at a good fart story.

By the end of this program I experienced so many jolts of wisdom that my body began to feel alive again. And with the same excitement and fear that Dr. Frankenstein must've felt, my family and friends have watched my reanimation.

American author, Joan Didion, said, "We tell ourselves stories in order to live," as a way of explaining the importance of an individual's power to interpret life and digest the world. The Build a Rainbow program instills that in both teachers and students through memoir writing. We defined memoir at La Plaza as "a discovery that makes you—you." And in the past two months, I have discovered the power within me that I thought was lost.

I know there will still be challenging days in which I will have to battle my depression, but now I also know not to end my story before it's over, that even when I can't change the situation, I can still decide my reaction, and most importantly, that laughter really is the best medicine. And in the words of Frankenstein's creature, "Beware; for I am fearless, and therefore powerful."

Anton T.

Age 9, Saint Florian

My Best Day Ever

I remember my best day ever. I got to ride my scooter. I rode it in my front yard. It has a long pole the bar its stop the scooter. I also played video games on my best day ever. I have Minecraft that I play on Xbox.

Georgia

We went to Macon, Georgia with grandpa and granny, Wendy, and Jennifer. We stayed in a house. We were at April's house. It was dark when we got there. We sleep there. We played ball. They watched videos. They watched YouTube.

The Best is Homemade

My favorite food is macaroni and cheese. It tastes good. It's yellow and crescent. Granny makes mac and cheese. It's got cheese on it. We eat it with dinner. We have it with green beans, mashed potatoes, and chicken. My mommy eats it with me. The best mac and cheese doesn't come in a box, it is homemade.

Ivan R.

Age 13, La Plaza

I Am...

I am a son and a brother. I am a son to my father and mother, my father is tall and a little chubby and he is a construction worker and I am also a student, minor, and uncle, and my mom is a little shorter than she has black hair and a great cook, and I got 2 nephews and 1 niece my 2 nephews names are Cameron and Nathan. Cameron is special he has a condition but I don't know what it is all I know that it involves asthma, and my other nephew Nathan is barely 1 years old but he is half Mexican and black.

Soccer All-Star

I see myself as a soccer player (professional) because I felt like that when I saw my brother play at one of his games
I remember when I saw a '57 Bel Air in the parking lot
I remember when I used to put his equipment on the bench so he can get ready. We used to race down the hill to the bench. Then when I turned around to put down his equipment. I won the race. I saw his friend. Then I saw him doing the rainbow. I would see him practicing.
I see myself as an allstar soccerfield
I'm gonna have kids. I'm gonna have 2 field.

The Rollercoaster

It had started when the fair had opened close to my house me and my family wanted to go because it was our first time at that one and we left around 7'oclock and we got to the parking lot and we saw this huge ride and it was going to be my first time on it my brother has been on something that was related to it so he wasn't scared but I was scared just by looking at it and hearing people scream so we got to the booth to get the bracelet to get on every ride but we had gotten tickets instead so my brother had asked me to get on with him so I hesitated for a while then he was like my role model at the time so I had to say yes so we got on.

My brother had asked me to be on the roller coaster that looks like 2 hammers being tossed like back and forth and so we got on one though I kinda didn't want to and he asked me and I hesitated for a while then I had said yes even though I was scared and still got on the ride.

Drop Tower and Sunscreen

I remember my stomach dropping and people screaming and me saying cuss words in my head when they are crazy. I can see other rides and people in line and screaming cars in the parking lot and can feel the clouds and when you least suspected it you drop down fast, it feels right after it feels like they might do it again but you really want to get off and the colors were green, red, purple, and at the very top there was a finish lap flag. Me and family went to the food location and we went to order and I saw the weirdest thing. There was a family having Ziploc bags and putting the free sunscreen in the bags so they ripped a hole and were putting it on and taking them home.

Dana S.

Age 13, Saint Florian

Making Friends

When I walked to the doors I was scared and wanted to go home. I didn't know what class I was supposed to go to. Then I started walk through the hallway and saw all the teachers. So, I went to the last class because it was close to the park. Then the teacher asked me what was my name? When I told her she said I could go in the classroom. When I went in class everyone was playing but I didn't want to play so I took a seat. I sat in the back. No one was at the table so I didn't think no one would sit at the table. Then she came in and asked everyone to get in the chairs. Then a lot of kids sat at my table and was talking too much. The kids that were doing all the talking was the bad kids. The other kids were scared of these kids. So I got out my chair and told them to shut up. Then the room went silent. Then the teacher told me to come to her. Then I went and she said to flip my card to red and go to the office. She had called before I had got there. Then the ladies that was there said she have been waiting on me to get there. Since I was in trouble I had to eat by myself in lunch. Then they sent me back to class and we went outside. Then I started talking to people while I was on the swings. The I started being friends with people. Then they yelled and said time to go in.

The Writer

I am 13.
I would teach people how to keep going and don't stop writing
My mom is my helper
My mom helped me with everything in writing
My favorite story was a scary story in 5th grade

Loss

When I was eight or nine my great grandma had died. I didn't really know her that much. I only seen her five times. The last time I seen her was when they were coming to get her body. The only time I seen her was when my grandma used to go to her house. Two years later my best friend died. He had got shot in the back of his head. He didn't die right away. He could've still been on Earth. He would've not been the same person that he was. His mother would have to teach him everything over. He loved to play football. His mother pulled the plug and he died.

Elyjah M.

Age 9, Saint Florian

Bus Trip

When I got home from school, my bus stopped in the middle of the road to see what was going on in my neighborhood. Mr. Roger told me that the maintenance was putting pavement on the road to make it easier to drive on. I guess the road was really bumpy and someone made a complaint about it. I just hoped they didn't get it on my house because my mom paid some guys to paint our house white since the walls were a mess. So my bus driver pulled up in the grass and opened the door right then and there. I tripped and fell on the grass, I heard the whole bus shake with laughter. Even Mr. Roger was laughing. I ran home and just started on my homework.

Getting My Roshes

I remembered when my sister and I went to the shoe store, and got these really cool Roshes. They were green at the bottom and grey at the top with black shoelaces. When we got home from Finish Line, I showed my sister the shoes and she said, "They're beautiful." The reason why I got the shoes was because my other shoes were getting too small for me, so my mom said, "I'll buy you some new shoes." My sister took me to her friend's baby shower and after the baby shower, we were going to go get the shoes. But the baby shower was so long, and my feet were starting to hurt. But on the bright side, we played games like Smell the Diaper, where we had to guess what kind of chocolate was in the diaper. And after that the people played intro's of song with the word baby in it, and we had to guess what song it was and who it was made by. Of course, I didn't win, but somebody else did. I think they won a really cool wine glass, but I don't drink wine. So it would be really weird if I got it. But that's a different story so I'll get back to the shoe story. When we left we when straight for Washington Square Mall and made our target Finish Line, and ran right to it. Then once we got to the store, the shoes were waiting for me on the glass plate. I picked them up and asked for the maintenance to help me buy them. I was excited to put them on.

Conversations that Run in Circles

I remember when it was the second to last day of school and it was pouring outside and I got off of the bus but I didn't have my key to my house. But luckily my sister and her friend was there with his car. So, they brought me into the car. After that we waited for my mother to arrive. It took a long time for her to get there so we just watched the rain soak people's heads. I saw a bag of rice on the dashboard with a phone battery drying in it.

"What happened to your battery?" I asked.

"It got wet so I'm waiting for it to dry out." She replied. Half an hour later Jalynne, my sister got there. My sister Darynne, texted Jalynne to unlock the door. So, when she unlocked the door Darynne got out of the car with an umbrella. Her friend and I were left back. After a moment of waiting we jumped out of the car and dashed to the front door of my house.

When we went in the house, Darynne asked me where my phone was. I zoomed upstairs and snatched my phone from the charger. I slid down the bannister like I was riding a rollercoaster.

"Here's my phone." I said, panting. She grabbed the phone from my hand and tore the back plating off. Taking the battery and sliding it into hers she flipped the power switch ON. "Hey, why'd you take my battery out?!" I shouted, angrily.

"My phone isn't working and I don't feel like waiting for it to dry out." She answered. I was so mad. Losing my battery meant I lost my phone and I couldn't play my favorite games.

"How am I supposed to wake up in the morning without my alarm?!" I reasoned.

"Get an alarm clock." She sassed.

"With what money?" I continued. This conversation could run in circles and circles and circles, I thought.

Corrie Herron

Lead Instructor, La Plaza and Saint Florian

Making a Difference

During our second session of La Plaza, we were asked to write about an issue we see in the world and how we would change it. Being an educator, the obvious issue for me was our education system. I see, almost on a daily basis, how we are failing our children. Seeing how I've only spent a short amount of time teaching, it was appalling that I was able to produce pages about specific students and how they are strong examples of our inadequate education system. I wrote, becoming more and more furious as I let myself remember each child that couldn't read, write, spell, use a comma. The first half of my writing went on until I couldn't think about these stories anymore. They were becoming too much.

When it came time to write a solution my hand stopped, my mind froze. I had nothing to say. I could write a novel about the issues we have, but I could not produce a single sentence on how to fix this hideous problem. I felt I was no better than those making the policies that were miserably failing. If I couldn't come up with a solution, how could I criticize those for trying? I slowly reasoned with myself that there is not a clear solution, an answer key to all the problems. Each child is different and each story is different. Upon accepting this answer, I realized there is something I can do to make a difference—I can allow these children to own their stories; I can accept that each child is different from the one sitting next to him or her; and I can give them a voice.

That's what this program does every summer—we give the unheard a platform to tell their stories. We can't fix everything and we can't teach the children everything they need to know in order to be successful, but we can try. I'm proud to say that I help these children tell their stories. I feel accomplished to know the public can see, hear, and try to understand how these children live their lives. As their tiny hand press pencil to paper, I feel immense happiness in knowing we are helping fix this problem, one word at a time.

Javier P.

Age 13, La Plaza

I Am…

I am Javier P.-L., Jr.
My name means named after my father
I am Mexican, soccer player, Jr.
I wonder about the future
I taste pizza
I smell of the fresh food my mom made
I feel my dog fur
I want money
I was crazy
I will be robotics engineers
I feel weak when I get up in the morning

Dodgeball

First day of school in third period it was time for gym. Our teacher's name was Mr. B. He stood up and said "Today we are playing Dodgeball," I was scared and not sure if there was going to be someone better than me and will throw a dodgeball to my face. When we got to the gym I picked up the dodgeball and threw it to the middle of the gym. We split into 2 groups. I did not know nobody in there. So I was almost the last to get picked. When we started I ran for the middle of the gym and threw the first ball. BOOM—hit in the chest. The reason I got the first hit was because I got a baseball throwing hand. Funniest moment was when somebody got hit on the face. In 15 min. it was time for lunch. We were all tired. Playing with people. After lunch we played in the small gym. This time we used half the balls. We made new teams. We were going to play backboard. When I have kids I am going to teach them how to play dodgeball without getting hit in the face. Looking into the future of Chito Frito, aka Javier, will teach kids how to throw like a boss.

Desmond R.

Age 13, Saint Florian

Mom's Famous Chicken

Came home to a greasy house
All I could smell is my mom famous chicken
I saw the grease everywhere
Grease bubbles popping out
Pop Pop Ssst Aww they pop on me
As I bit into the chicken the grease
came into mouth all warm
The skin I eat first
Every time bite into the meat heaven comes my way.

Running from Bats

I remember when I was around the corner from my house and I was on my way back home. I tripped over a rock. I was flying. I fell on the ground and was sliding like a penguin. My cloth was dirty and to this day I can't get the stains out. I got up and they start to laugh at me. So I laugh with them. Me and my cousin was runnin' home Because Bats was everywhere. I got home around 11 o'clock. I went to bed.

Tickle Monster

I was over my auntie's house and every night we always play a game when we go to bed. She always said are you ready for the tickle monster, Then she would go silent we would always get scared. She pop up and we was screaming like girls. I never been so scared I almost peed in my pants. But Kian got scared so she turned on the lights. So we went to bed with laugh on our hearts.

Horse Back Riding

I remember when I went to horse back riding. My mom and I went to Fort Benjamin Harrison Park to the horses. So I waited till they call my name, so they did and she pick me with Hotshot a horse that I fell in love with. Hotshot is an all brown with black and a little white patch on his neck. When we started on our trail ride we went in the woods. We went over the stream and it was beautiful. At the end I want to buy the horse. But before we start with that, the funniest was when the horse Boo Boo was sneezing then my mom got scared that it would get on her. So I was laughing my heart out.

Collaborative Poem

Concord

Cinnamon

It reminds me of cinnamon cookies
and snicker doodles,
pine cones at Christmas
and toast at my grandma's house.

It smells like cinnamon applesauce
and cinnamon raisin bread
and cinnamon Yankee Candles.

When you open a lid,
it looks like smoke.

It reminds me of my grandma's cooking
and all of the women in my family,
their overcrowded spice cabinets.
It reminds me of the school lunches
my mom packed.

And that's that.

Counselor Mya T.

Saint Florian

Eyelashes

One day at my old job I was wearing false eyelashes. And my coworker who was kind of ditzy anyway, asked me, "Where do they get the hair from for the false eyelashes from?" and I Told her horses. She said, "Really?" and I said, "Yes!" She said, "How?" and I said, "You cut off the horse tails and measure how long you want them and glue them on." She believed me it was so funny. I Told all of my coworkers and my bosses because it was too funny not to tell.

Wait 12 Counts

The first time I sang in front of people, I was so nervous. I tried everything I could to get out of it. But it was for a grade so I had to do it. I remember everyone in Ms. West's Private Lesson class sat on stage in a semi circle. And one by one everyone sang. Then it was my turn! My hands broke out in a cold sweat. I got a little dizzy. I can't turn back now. Left foot slightly forward. Wait 12 counts. Breathe. Then words came out. Once I started to sing I felt that the world was my oyster and I owned the stage. From that day forward preforming became the love of my life.

The first time I sang on the street for money, I was so nervous. We were in Tuscany, Italy. At first I jokingly started to sing a camp song. But then I switched to an Italian aria. Then I switched to "Wade in the Water." And people loved it. I made five Euros that night. I was singing in front of this man's apartment. He came outside and looked @ me and kept his patio door opened the whole time. But the most memorable thing about it was an Italian woman sang as she put money in my hand. It was Awesome!

Enas H.

Age 11, Saint Florian

Tackling Fears like a Professional Linebacker

I remember the time I learned to ride a bike. My dad had been trying to teach me for over a year. Fail after fail after fail.

Then one day my dad packed up my bike and took me to an old abandoned building.

"What are we doing here," I asked.

"You're going to learn to ride your bike," said my dad. My dad took my bike out of the back of his truck and told me to get on. I was a little nervous about learning to ride my bike. I had seen some clips of the Tour De France race and how bloody and dangerous biking could be, but with some encouragement from my dad I tackled my fears like a professional linebacker and got on my bike.

After I got on, my dad gently pushed me around and around the building. Every once and a while I would ask, "How am I doing" and my dad would said, "Great." Then one time I asked and I heard no reply. I asked again, too afraid to look behind me. Then as I came around the building, I saw my dad had stopped pushing me and I didn't even notice. Then my dad pulled out a tennis racquet and started playing wall ball with a tennis ball on the building as I rode around the building on my bike.

We came back to the building for the next month or so to help me perfect my art, one time I almost got hit by a semi-truck coming into the parking lot. Soon I was proudly able to say I could ride my bike.

Health 101

I remember when I got my scar right next to my left eye. It was just a few weeks ago to be exact. I was just playing tag with friends when tragedy struck. I was running backwards to get my start. The tagger ran right in front of me. Then when I turned around to start running, the side of my face slammed into a pole. I was a little dazed, and walked around the playground for a few seconds. Then William walked up to me and cracked a joke. I took my hand off of where I got hit, and blood came down like Niagara Falls. I went right to a counselor and went inside. I went to the bathroom and applied pressure to the wound with a wet paper towel (that's some Health 101). Then I looked at my shirt and it was completely stained with blood. I tried to wipe it off but it just made it worse. I got some Band-Aids on it and went outside and sat on the bench. Then everybody started swarming me like ants swarming the old chocolate bar under the picnic table. Everybody kept on asking the same question. "What Happened!? What Happened!?" At first I told the whole story, but then it got molded into the same old classic answer, "I ran into a pole." We called my dad and he picked me up to take me to the hospital. I kept on saying I'm sorry, because the price for that isn't cheap. I got to the hospital and, no surprise, I get stitches. The nurse put some stuff to numb my wound, but the doctor got there too late and the numbing cream wore off they had to put the painful kind in. They stuck a needle into my skin and put in some powerful numbing medicine. During the operation I felt the thread falling on my eyelid. When we got out of the hospital we went to the Original Pancake House. It hurt my scar a little bit. Then I got to Laze out the rest of the day. The next day I'm playing baseball. The good news of it all is that the blood came out of the shirt.

Jesus F.

Age 14, La Plaza

I Am a Saxophone

I like to play the saxophone because I saw a video on YouTube. A guy was playing a saxophone and he was playing so fast he was playing for 10 min. He was playing 5 songs so fast. I was so surprised. I was at my house in San Francisco, California. My cousin showed me this and I wondered how he did it. My cousin came from school with a saxophone. And he started playing it in my house and He played it. And I like how it sounds. I want to get to college and a marching band. And be a professional saxophone player. I love the saxophone. I will go around the world playing Jazz, worldwide.

Language

I first was in the U.S.A. I went to school I was going to 2nd grade and it was my first time to go to school in the U.S. I did not know what to do because everyone was speak English I did not speak English. I just speak Spanish and some kids speak English and Spanish. Some kids help me.

Friend or Foe

I was going to the second grade for the first time in my life at a new school and I was the new kid in school. I went to my first class and a boy was mean to me and he was eight years old and I was seven years old and he bully me for three to four weeks and he stop and he tell me to play soccer and he was my first friend in school.

Counselor Nichole

Saint Florian

Mr. Johnson's Class

I remember when I was in the 4th grade in Mr. Johnson's class. We had just come back from the restroom and I rushed back first and sat a tack in Mr. Johnsons chair so when he sat down he would jump up. So when everyone was back in class, I told Elvis and my friend Lisa what I had done so we sat and waited, and waited, and waited. It seemed like it took him forever to go sit down at his desk. So finally he went to his desk and we started asking questions so he wouldn't look down in the chair and see the tack so finally he sat down and nothing happened. We all looked at each other like "what happened." Then he got up and when he walked by, the tack was stuck in his Brown polyester pants like it went in between his cheeks. The whole class started laughing so hard it was so so funny. Later I got called out to the hallway and got a paddle for it. Then it wasn't so funny anymore.

Lab Work

I remember playing a trick on my son Quenten. He is very scared of needles and I took him and his older brother Dominique to the Doctors for their yearly check-up. Dominique had to get blood work done so I had the doctors and the Lab techs to play along and tell Quenten that he had to get his blood drawn also. It was so funny watching him squirm in his chair. He was so ready to run. Remind you he was 17yrs old and a football player. So when they called his name, his eyes got so big he started pacing the floor and rubbing his hands and when he sat down he kept looking at the door like he was getting ready to run and really he was. Right when the lab Tech grabbed the rubber thing to put around his arm, we All started laughing and told him that we tricked him. You should've seen the sigh of relief on his face and all he could do was say, "I was getting ready to run out the door." I was laughing so hard I was crying and my stomach was hurting.

Caden D.

Age 6, Saint Florian

Cornbread

I had it as Miss Carla's, my teacher at daycare. Miss Carla cuts it into squares, and we eat it warm. Yellow on top, brown on the bottom. We eat it at lunch, sometimes I get two pieces when I ask nicely.

My mom makes cornbread, and so does dad.

I would eat it everyday.

CADEN

Calm, cool, careful
Awesome
Debonair
Encouraging
Nice

On Purpose

I was playing basketball and I fell. I tried to shoot the ball and I missed. Someone fouled me on the PlayStation. Someone jumped on my head. I was happy. I like being fouled. I went to the free throw line. I made that shot. I fouled the other team on purpose. I jumped right on their face. And then everyone went to the locker room and kicked everything. I was HAPPY! I only had 1 person on my team. I jumped and run around. Other team's ball. I fouled them again.

Playing with Carson

My friend Carson and I like to play tag. We play tag outside at school during recess. Sometimes Carson is faster than me, and sometimes I'm faster than Carson. Carson and I also play basketball. I am better playing basketball, but sometimes it's a tie. Carson is taller, but I'm faster.

I remember feeling happy because I like to pass and shoot. We play for a short time. After we play, we get our tickets for snacks.

My daddy keeps score for us.

Football

I lost my football player. I couldn't find him for a month. He went under the bed. My daddy found him. He put him in the toy box. I found him there. I felt happy and excited. I played with him in my bed. I rolled around and crushed Eli Manning. Eli Manning broke his arm. I pulled his hand back to pass and it broke. My nanny fixed it. She put tape on it. I was happy Eli Manning got hurt, because it was funny. I played with my toys.

I play football and basketball on the PlayStation. I scream in the living room because I made a touchdown or a goal. I play Pacers, and OKC Thunder, and North Carolina. I won. I foul all the time. I like to foul. I push people. Sometimes I sit on the couch and get off and get on the floor.

Armundo P.

Age 8, Saint Florian

Playing a Game

It was a big green field with a lot of people on it. Me had to run around the field 1 time. Next I had to do jumping Jacks and push ups. And then we had to stretch by putting one arm over the other arm. It was warm we were wearing football helmets, shoulder pads, and cleats. And we had to wear pants with cushions inside. The shoulder pads were much heavier than the helmet. We had to do races running and I won. We did bear claws. Then we started playing a game. I was on offense and defense, Everyone was cheering. I had to run all the way down field to tackle him. And We Won. And my team was the FIGHTING IRISH.

Special Soccer

I remember when I played soccer. It was the best day ever. I made friends. And it got easier and easier. I started to make points. I remember I was playing on my best friend's team and the score was 4 to 10. So Then when the game was over, we had to line up and go inside and my teacher had to do the password code to get inside and we too had drink from the water fountain. We lined back up and we went back to the classroom. It was so special because I was in the first grade and I made points and new friends. Outside, the field was big.

Bob Evans

My favorite food is pancakes, they're good. My dad took me to Bob Evans and I got pancakes and sausages. I go out my neighborhood turn right kept going forward for about 20 seconds and we arrive in Bob Evans parking lot. When we go in the door we get seated at the front table after my dad talks to his friends. He then orders me pancakes, sausage, eggs, and orange juice. My dad then orders himself coffee, pancakes, and eggs. While we are waiting for the food we wait patiently and go wash our hands in the washroom. Then the food comes. My dad cuts my pancakes and the sausages then he puts the ketchup on my hash browns and syrup on the pancakes and sausages and then I eat some times my dad calls me the pancake king.

Playing in Our Field

I remember when me and my sister were outside playing soccer. My sister kicked the ball so hard it went into the street. She had to go chase it and she got the soccer ball and ran in the neighbor's sidewalk and said, "Give me the ball," and she kicked the soccer ball up in the air. It went in to the neighbor's yard into the bushes. It was warm and in the summer. We laughed at her.

Jeremiah H.

Age 7, Saint Florian

Jordans

My favorite shoes is Jordans. Yellow and gray.
I wear them to church. When I walk they feel soft on my feet. I walked from home to church and they were soft. I feel cool in them. The Jordans are better than just Nikes. I'd be playing basketball and I'd scratch them up. I clean them and put them back in the box. My mom saw my shoes in the car and got my Jordans at Foot Locker. Me and my sister were dressing up together because she got the different Nike shoes. I told my mom can I put on my running shoes to play in and play Football. We play in the hot sun.

Quarterback

Me and my friend was playin' football 'cuz we had a game tomorrow. I can't go 'cuz I'll be late, but I'm the best quarterback anyway. Before the game starts we practice. My coach helps me. The quarterback threw the ball at the person and nobody didn't catch him and he scored a touchdown. I am a wide receiver and a quarterback. My team is the Eagles and my number is number 1. The final score is 35 to 25. We won. We won in only 10 minutes in the final quarter. My mom bought Gatorade and snacks after the game. Our uniforms are all blue.

Heat Vs. Pacers

I remember when my friend played football with me. Then we played a football game on the X-box. They had an X-box controller that's tight. We played 2K14. I was the Heat and my friend was the Lakers. I won because LeBron kept dunking on people. My brother likes the Heat, so he started playing and I was playing and my friend Jarrel came. We were in my room. It's all blue. It was sunny fun because I shot a 3. We play teams and then we got some more friends because it wasn't fair. It was Kevin, Hollis, DeShawn, Paul, and Anthony and Elijah. We got something to drink. It was a blue Gatorade. And then the game was over. The score was 28 to 37. We won. Our team was called The Heat, the other team called The Pacers and then we rode our bikes. My brother came over and asked to play a game.

Chase S.

Age 7, Saint Florian

Water Balloon Fight

One day my friend told me to go over to his house. He said he had nine water balloons but I thought that he was playing around but he ran to his porch but picked up the water balloons to throw them at me. I dodged first one but he got me with the second one so I got mad at him because he got two. So I hurried up and threw it at him. But he kept throwing them at me and my back was so wet and I wanted to catch him but then my face was so wet. I told my mom and now we get water balloons and we play this all the time. It feels good when you are hot. The End.

Riding a Bike

This is the story of the first time I try to ride a bike. Well I already had bike is just I was get too big so I rode it the rest of the day then the next day. I got ready for school then waited for the bus. And when I got home, I went to my room and my mom told me to go in to the kitchen and my Auntie Carin was in there so a couple hours later my keep my bother bike but he's too big for it now. So keep trying to ride but I finally got to ride the bike and keep cat using it to make sure I had it then a couple of days later my auntie had to leave I was sad and we was at the airport We went home.

Basketball Practice

I was with my Basketball coach he said I needed help with Dribbling with My left and right. Hand and that was at the end of practice. My mom told My brother to Help me. Then he was mad he kept arguing with My mom then a couple of Days later he was on punishment because he got in trouble at school. Then he wanted to Help Me with My Basketball.

Jeremiah E.

Age 12, Concord

Dad on a Mission

Dede, he likes basketball.
He plays basketball
with me in our driveway.
My dad always takes
me to the gym so
I can play basketball.
He teaches
me new skills, new
dribble moves and
cross overs. He used
to play Center.
He also takes me to
the weight room.
He lifts weights
with me and that's
why I am so strong.
When he lifts curls
he looks so strong,
like a gorilla
banging on his chest.

"Café Terrace on the Place du Forum" *By Vincent Van Gogh*

I see people in the dark eating.
I see about 21 people
getting ready to eat.
The pebbled ground
looks like crops
growing. The time of day
is night time looking up at
the sky it looks like
it has about 30 moons/stars.
There is a dark building in the city/town
tall and looks like houses.
So many yellow/orange
lights in the town

Eco Lab Trip

OK here we go again
just went to the eco lab I
saw a winter beaver
Den. The Den was
brown and was
made out of sticks/mud etc.
Delphinium I saw
is a Native flower. There
is a pink flower called
milk weed, or a swamp.
milk weed. Monarch
butterflies eat the
milk/swamp weed
to get poisonous. Me
standing on a log the
Log is big and is brown.
I had saw a turtle
on a log In the pond
it was little.

Angeles S.

Age 9, Saint Florian

Mexico

I went on a mission trip to help a family in need. When we got to the site we saw the family, it was a mother, a daughter, and baby on the way. We had 3 days to build this house on the 1st day we painted, drilled, hammered, and even sawed. It was finally the last day. The house was finished, the furniture was put in, we gave the keys away, gave words of encouragement, and left. After we left everybody wanted to do this all over again. It was really amazing to see how just building them a house can bless them so much! I want to do this a billion times more!

I Remember...

I remember when me and my friend Lalah went to the pool. When we got to the pool our neighborhood was there (P.S. Tia had been in trouble with the neighborhood for a while!)! So when we got to the pool Tia ran up to us and said we said hi! We said hi back and walked over to the pool chairs to get settled. We got into the pool and said it was cold. Tia jumped in and said with an attitude, "IT'S NOT COLD!" We said, "Okay! Okay! You don't have to be so mean about it!" She said, "You're not the boss of me." We try to make friends with her but it always fires back at us. Even though she is mean to us we try to kill her with kindness.
THE END

Bleeding to Death

I remember when I got a bad, bad scar. My Mom was doing something in the house so I decided to go get my bike out of the garage. So I got it out and started riding it (P.S. I had sandals on!). I was going at a decent speed and then it happened. My foot slipped off of my pedal, my sandal flipped off, and I am on the cement ground bleeding to death! I sat there for a minute and then I started crying and screaming. My sister came outside and started laughing because she thought I was kidding around but I wasn't.

Malia Sandberg

Lead Instructor, La Plaza and Saint Florian

The Blank Space between the Blue Lines

I am honored to complete my second year as an intern with the Build a Rainbow writing program. 50 plus kids shuffle in on any given morning; chatting, twirling, stomping, laughing, running, squirming and singing. At 9:00 AM these kids are ready for life. Our challenge as writing instructors is to convince them to focus the same energy and enthusiasm into a unique piece of writing. The kids approach the task in a variety of ways. Some dive head first and hardly come up for breath the whole hour. Head down, hand moving, they only stop when their pencil gets too dull to write another word. Others are more hesitant; they slowly write their name, tap their pencils, and stare intimidated at the blank space between the blue lines on their paper. Stuck, unsure, and insecure is how most of us approach writing, especially about ourselves. We push each of our students to overcome this intimidating task, because we know they have valuable stories, something only they carry, and something too good to miss. We ask the students to write stories that are true and meaningful. They require thought, courage, and honest reflection to share. Each of the students this year took on the challenge and in doing so they became authors. My favorite part of our program is the eagerness to share a student holds when they have created a piece of piece of writing they are proud of. The same students who once felt threatened by the blank piece of paper, now hold it dearly, stamped with a story that is uniquely their own. The children realize that their stories are worth being heard, and they invite others to listen. As a reader, I hope you accept the invitation into the lives of our authors. With zest for life the authors of this book chat, twirl, stomp, laugh, run, squirm and sing their stories throughout these pages. Courageously and honestly, the kids share memories of laughter, hurt, loss, and joy. They share stories of who they are, where they come from, and what they love. In return, I hope you too take on the blank paper challenge. Tackle it honestly and courageously, trusting that your story is worth sharing too.

Breanna N.

Age 13, Saint Florian

Scar on the Parking Lot

Running to the bus, ready to tour the number 10 fire station when it happened—a trip, then a fall. I jumped off the curb like I do in every setting. I guess my legs gave in. I went head first and I tumbled. As I laid there I noticed the laugh and disrespect that pass by. I also noticed the care that stopped by my side. It felt like hours before help came to sit me up and examine me. I felt the ache in my side and I just knew there were scars on my knees. As I sat up I didn't even want to look at my knee, I knew it was way too serious. As I eased my hands off of my face I seen the blood and the white of my leg. Then I looked at my left knee and it was the typical scrape. On my right knee the firefighter was rubbing an ointment on it so it wouldn't get infected. I jumped, thinking it would sting, but I didn't feel much. After that my knee was wrapped and taped, but I still wasn't ready to get up. The only problem was I didn't have a choice. The parking lot isn't the best place to sit. I got up with the assistants of a firefighter and a counselor and limped back to the bus.

Painting Our Nails

I remember the summer of 2013 when I got my nails done on the cruise ship I was on. I was with my friend who at first wasn't up for the idea. She wasn't into my style of bright neon colors. She was into the dark colors. My granddad booked the appointment for the next day at 10 in the morning. The next day I woke up and heard knocks at the door. It was 9:55. I opened the door and she was at the door dressed. I looked at my iPod and ran in the restroom. I unwrapped my hair while brushing my teeth. I put my shorts on and put my hoodie on. We ran to the salon and made it in at 10:10. The ladies still took us to the back to do our nails. We didn't tell my granddad we were late, because we knew what he was going to say. My friend went first and she got a sparkly black. At first she just wanted black, but I made a deal with her. I said if you get sparkles, I'll get a dark color. She finally let the lady paint her nails. The lady was from Jamaica so we couldn't understand a lot of what she was saying. We were there for about an hour waiting for the paint to dry.

Trying Squid

My first time trying squid was my first and my last time eating it. Me, my dad, my stepmom, and my 2 brothers went to Teppanyaki. My dad brought a bread-covered piece of food to the table. Along with the plate he brought a cup of sriracha. He told my brothers to try it but they said no. Then my dad told me to try it. I was hesitant at 1st then he said if I ate it he would give me $20. I thought it was chicken, so I was wondering why he would give me that much for eating a piece of chicken. I didn't bother to ask the question so I dipped the breaded piece of food in the sriracha sauce. I put it in my mouth and it slithered down my throat. Then everyone started to laugh. I asked why and they said, "You just ate squid!" Then I got mad and went to the restroom.

2 years later I finally got my money.

The Performance

Getting ready to perform, putting my lipstick on, then my nose started to bleed. "Not now," I thought, this was nosebleed number 3 in 2 days. We were ready to walk out of the star Room when I grabbed the whole roll of tissue. As we walked out of the room I dropped the tissue by the door and walked out. We lined up on the right side of the court ready to dance. When they announced our name I walked out then ran to my spot. The music started and we started dancing. I heard Mya yelling my name. Then as I walked off the court, I tripped trying to wave.

Chelsey H.

Age 12, Concord

This is Me

This is me I'm hardworking
Remember this of me.

Big Sister. Amazing daughter and granddaughter
Standing tall. Hard and strong for what I believe
in.

Strong but Shy on the outside. Inside
I try to hide.

But remember me when you
Ask How to do something cause
I am the one who knows you
can!

The Turtle

We saw it diving. We watched
quietly as it climbed on the log

the sun light Glistening on the
wet hard back shell

everyone started to talk

the peace and quiet slowly
drifted away

the turtle Dove again.

Growth

As the Birds cheep and the crickets
rattle it sounds like a love
song.

And when the big thick, sweet
Juicy raspberries hang down

I'm like a tad pole rushing
through the thick muddy
puddle soon to be a full
grown Frog.

High Land Lakes!

As I return
to High Land Lakes camp
I realize how lucky I am I sing and celebrate
I'm away from home! Finally,
the smell of nature is so refreshing
From the smell of gasoline, rushing cars on the road.
I see old friends and hear laughter
we all play a game
called ninja. We have our first night party
The water in the pool is as clear as fresh air
and all the noise mutes down
as I dive in. It's so peaceful.

I finally get home sick
but as the marshmallows slowly roast on the fire
on the last night I smile, knowing
that I had a great time.

Amari S.

Age 13, Saint Florian

End of a Bad Friendship

One day I lost my best friend. We had gotten into an argument because she was hurting me and making bad decisions. She was hurting me by causing drama in my life and mixing my words. She made bad decisions by smoking and doing inappropriate things with boys. I had her back no matter what but she didn't have mine. I couldn't take the hurt any longer so I yelled to her, "We are NOT best friends! You hurt me too many times! I trusted you and I cared for you like my own sister!" I looked at her face... and walked away. My heart was beating as fast as a lion chasing its prey. I went home and cried my eyes out because I had once again lost a close friend. But till this day I will never regret my decisions and I have a wide variety of other close friends. It was as if she never was my best friend. Being best friends was like chewing nails. I care more about the relationship than she did. Best friendship is a two way street if one is trying and the other isn't, it's not good.

The Broken Headphones

A time I was mad is when my new headphones had broken. I was so annoyed because I paid good money for them. Plus they were purple my favorite color. I waited forever for them.... I WANTED THOSE HEADPHONES. I wanted them to listen to music...and so I could shut the whole world out. My mom laughed because she said I didn't need them, which made me more mad. But then I got over it.

Cilantro Fiascos

A time when I laughed so hard is when I was eating out at Houlihan's. My dad had eaten some cilantro. Which he hates. He spit it out on ground and said, "That stuff tastes like booty crust." My mom, sister, nephew, and I all laughed so hard! It sounded like a hyena laughing. It made my sister choke on her pop. After I stopped laughing my stomach and ribs ached.

Crab Legs

When I went to Journey, (a restaurant with cultural foods) with my mom, dad, and sister. I ate my favorite food, crab legs. The spiny hard shell hurt against my fingers. I got the cracker and cracked it. I slivered it out and dipped it in the butter. "Ummm..." My mouth started singing and my stomach mourned for more. I ate them all and I left happy. I fell asleep in the car and I dreamed of my delectable food. That's my favorite food because it good and taste like Heaven.

Joseph Michael Bell

On Thursday, June 19th, 2014 I heard some very bad news. My PawPaw had died on Father's Day. He passed from a heart attack. The very evil and hatred thing about it is that other family members knew and didn't tell us. I cried for hours and I was furious of the actions of my family. Then I realized that he wouldn't have wanted me to be sad or mad. My mom, dad, and sisters had to learn how to think of good memories like how he held food in his mouth and saved it for later. He saves chunks in his cheek and will still be eating on it 10 minutes later. Or his hilarious laugh. It sounds like an engine trying to start. I Love him dearly and he will be missed greatly. Now he is with his wife MawMaw. They are together and healthier than Before.

R.I.H.
PawPaw

Jeremiah K.

Age 6, Saint Florian

Turning My Lip Down

I remember when my grandma died. I think she died in 2011. She passed away. She was exhausted. She had cancer and she was really sick. Me and my brother were there, and my cousin, and my mom, and everybody that I know! She had one of those white things on her face when she died. Everybody took a picture of her. She was in her casket. I felt sad, everybody that I know was sad. I showed a sad face by turning my lip down.

My Grandma

I remember my grandma when I was a baby. She had a boyfriend, but now he has a new girlfriend. She was 76. She was funny because she was telling jokes. I remember her on the first Christmas, too. It was really fun. All of my cousins, my aunties, and uncles, and my mom were there. Grandma sang all of the Christmas songs—Jingle Bells, the reindeer with the shiny nose, I don't remember the others. I was like three or two years old. I like to hug her so much.

Nikes: My Favorite Shoes

I remember my favorite shoe was my Nikes. They're light blue and the strings are black and almost on the bottom is white. I wore those shoes everywhere and I almost wore them everyday. We was playing basketball sometimes in these shoes. Somebody was wearing the same shoes, but they were grey and pink. Her name was Camaya. I didn't feel nothing that she had the same shoes. I stopped wearing the shoes because they were getting dirty. I felt sad that I couldn't wear them anymore.

The Fart

I remember when somebody made me laugh real hard It was a counselor. When me and the other Jeremiah were by him, he farted real, real loud so that all the windows busted. Me and the other Jeremiah cracked up. So funny. We smelled the fart. It smelled like rotten eggs that a skunk pooipooed on.

The Dolphin Show

I remember when I went to the dolphin show at the Indianapolis Zoo. My mom, my brother, and me went on my field trip. My sister didn't go—she wasn't born yet. I remember the dolphin jumped and ate the fish and it caught a blue and red ball. It was fun to watch it. It was tight; it was cool. I wish I could be a dolphin and a person, like Sharkboy.

Austin S.

Age 12, Concord

My Cat

My cat reminds me of a soft cover just getting
done coming out of the dryer. I am not afraid
to cross his path because to me, he's good
luck. His black style with blond markings
helps me find him. His relative loves to play
with him and they are good companions. My cat
is a sleeping machine and his favorite spot
to sleep is on my sister's bed. Now he lies
across the yard, asleep for good.

Moth

As beautiful as a butterfly,
as nasty as a rat, with my
hot rod wings and dead skin. With my
big head and small body. As curvy as
a pretzel with its fuzzy body. I fly around
until I'm done and then I lie down till
the very next day. Now I'm gone, dead and
out on display.

Jewelweed

The water, glistening through the leaves.
Every drop makes the plant look even more
beautiful. The best looking plant I have
ever seen, is now in my mind.

Swimming

I walk into the breezing water park with my
family. There was fun water slides and a cold
pool. My sister ran straight to the sprinklers
and I leaped into the pool with my brother.
My mom went to the chair to get a tan, with
my dad. I really thought about getting on the
water slides with my brother. We went to
the slides and we had a race. I rushed down
doing my trick, the relaxation, while my brother
laid down to go fast. Curving and turning I went until
finally, we went back to the pool. I felt the
excitement and the rush. We left the pool
wishing we could go to the pool next week.

Jeffery C., Jr.

Age 7, Saint Florian

Pranksters

Me and my cousin were watching this one funny video. This man he slipped and then he fell into the pool. My cousin started laughing so hard that he fell out of his chair. I picked him back up but I was laughing. Then we both sat down and started watching TV. And then we got bored and were going to wake up his sister. We poured water on her face. It was cold water, and she woke up and started chasing after us. She said, "I'm out of breath." And then after that, my auntie went over to my grandma's house

Rachel Johnson
Student Teacher, Concord and Saint Florian

Learning to Tell My Own Story

There are some people in this world who have to write. I believe that I am one of those people. I need to write to remember the most mundane and to forget the most embarrassing. I need to write to seek and to share information. I need to write when I'm lonely, when I'm sad, and when I've had the best day ever. I need to write to get my thoughts out of my head and to make sense of them on the page.

Over this last year, I've had to write for many reasons other than these. I've had to write lesson plans to teach in the classroom. I've had to write résumés to give to potential employers. I've had to write an undergraduate thesis to obtain my degree. These types of writing have been difficult, yet nothing short of rewarding, but in the midst of writing my story in these forms for others, I've ignored writing my story for myself. And this has not been without consequence.

I've spent this last year coming to believe that the best teachers are those who practice their discipline outside of the classroom. And while I believe that, I haven't been living it. Maybe it's because I'm in a period of transition where I'm neither fully a student nor fully a teacher, as I will begin student teaching in an eighth grade language arts classroom on the north side of Indianapolis this fall. In this time of transition, I've made excuse after excuse for why I can't write. After a day of writing for others, writing for myself sounds like a chore. Instead of doing the one thing that I know deep down will help me to make sense of my ever-changing world, I shy away from it.

I was doing the same thing with our prompts for the Writers Center. I dreaded creating models that I could share with students, waiting until late the night before or even early the morning of to sit down and put my stories on paper. None of the prompts really spoke to me like I felt they should. None, that is, until our writing topic for the day at Concord was to compose a poem about a teacher. Partially out of guilt for not submitting a model sooner, I sat down and wrote the following poem about an experience I had the first week of summer:

"What do you do?"
she asks as our legs dangle
into the clear blue pool water.
"I'm an eighth grade
teacher," I lie,
looking up into the sun so
she'll ask no further
questions about a life I don't
yet lead. And when she
doesn't I still feel guilt, not
for lying to a total
stranger, but for expecting
my kids to be honest and
humble while I can't keep
my own story straight.

The next day, my poem appeared on the handout. Dylan sat across from me at Concord and, looking back and forth between me and the paper, asked first "What's your first name again?" only to be followed by, "Miss Rachel, what's your *last* name?" out of utter disbelief that I could be a published poet alongside some of the greats of contemporary poetry.

So there I had it. A reason to write: an audience with whom to share my writing. I was even finally living out what I professed to be one of the most important lessons anyone could ever know about teaching. But even after this successful lesson, I still struggled to sit down and write.

I struggled because some of the most important writing that we will ever do isn't meant to be shared.

We had just finished our last session with the 6-9-year-olds at Saint Florian and the 10-13-year olds were bee lining to their tables that, for the first time all summer, didn't have nametags sitting on them. One of the 10-year-olds with whom I enjoy writing had stomped into the classroom and sat with his head down at the back. I was passing out snacks and made a mental note to come back to him, but my plan was interrupted by one of the other interns: "Miss Rachel, Chris needs to talk with you."

I sat down to listen as Chris explained how awful his day had been so far. Our snack break was quickly coming to a close, so I suggested that we write down what had happened after the introduction to the day's lesson. I turned back to the front to listen, but my attention was drawn back to Chris by the sound of ripping paper.

"What are you doing?" I asked Chris as he continued ripping a sheet of notebook paper into smaller and smaller pieces.

"You told me to write down my story. Now I'm ripping it up so I won't dwell on it," Chris stated matter-of-factly as he scooped up the papers to throw away.

All summer, I had felt like Chris needed me to help tell his story. We made deals where if I wrote down four sentences, which Chris told me is the amount that makes a paragraph, then he would write down four sentences. Once we would finish the story, we would read back through it. I would add in two details, then he would add in two more details to enhance his story. I didn't see what Chris wrote on that paper before he threw it away, but Chris didn't need me to help him write that story. It was a story he needed to tell for himself.

It wasn't until Chris waved as he walked out of the classroom that I realized he had taught me more about what it means to write in this one day than I had probably helped him in our eight sessions. In that moment, the teacher became the student again, and that's the way it ought to be. If Chris could use the written word to make sense of his life in transition, surely I could do the same.

Here's to the beginning of an Indianapolis young adult learning to write about her own life because of the youth she has encountered who are brave enough to write about theirs.

Anthony W.

Age 12, Saint Florian

The Game

It was our 7th game and we lost bad in the first half we had our best players out and our play were good and our defense was good and by the time the second half we were up by 10 and I was happy that we were winning and I was in the game I said that I was going to make more than ten point and I did but the final score was 28 to 44.

Best Day Ever

I was waking up at 7:00 AM and then from 7:00 to 7:10 I got ready and went to go pick up my friend we went to the park and we went swimming. We went down the side that turned sharply and dives you straight into the water. Then we did back flips in the water to see who could do them better. I won because I used to do gymnastics. I learned from my cousin and he told me to jump and lean backward. The water was cold because I Had to get out the water to Help my mom. When we were there my little cousins came after that we played for 5 more minutes so when we went Home. We had pizza and all the snacks we had got Home at 6:00 we got to the pool at 8:00. 11:00 to 12:00 we went to McD's. Well after we had our food we wash up and watched TV and went to sleep all four of us.

THE END

"Mercy"

The story of what happened when I got the scars on my hands happened when my friend Melissa Dug her nails in my hands. I had said, "Let's play mercy." I had start to win and she had start to dig. "Aw that hurt," I said, then I push her harder. The more I push, the more she dug. Then she grab my other hand and started to dig and then I push harder and harder that she yell. We were Both hurt But we Did not stop. Then I got my hand Back and push her. She yell, "Mercy."

THE END

Javier G., Jr.

Age18, La Plaza

Lane Won't Stay (life path)

8:00 was the time I was born
My mom didn't know what she was waiting for
My father wasn't there for us
If I was able to talk, I would tell Javier there no but
Mom Gave me everything while my father put his little brother 1st
he told my mother that "family first" but he was married with her
it like saying his brother is over me
I knew my life wasn't right and I wasn't the guy I was supposed to be
15 years later I found the truth
I was everyday lost didn't know what to do
I asked my mother for the truth
I didn't took my time to think before I get my life srew
I talked to my father on the phone once, never hung up saying "I love you"
he lied to me, he tried to set up my mom and me
I hate him till death, that why his daughter hate me
I understood everything until I was 17
If I ran away, my life would've been worst than right now
without everyone Understanding me
My father is my forever enemy
I choice the right path after my mom change me 1st
I understand my mom and I are still hurt
but as long as we're still together, we'll be alright
Not only my mother change my path, god also got someone
to be put in my life
That person is my stepdad who is a father to me
cuz he's alway by mother side
If god never gave my mom and me my father (stepdad)
I wouldn't live in a big house, have a brother or sister
Would've be a real man and not the guy I am right now
I would've taught myself real life since I was little
Glad god gave my mom my father to change both of our life into where we are right now.

Who Am I?

I am Javier G., Jr.
I was named after my father who is a loser
I'm a Mexican but born in Chicago
I would've of been called Alfonso
I'm the 4th family gen. on both side (mom and stepdad)
but overall, I'm still the different kind of guy
I wonder if someone was looking like me
that the person I wanna meet
I could hear myself just like I was when I was in my past
but never heard myself just when I was with my dad
I could see my future making video games and some rap
I can't see it because the image is trap
I could feel the taste our my Mexican dinner from the food
I could tell the taste is gonna be good
but what I really feel in my head is struggle
that why I live my life single and not in a couple
all I want is money to cause good life value
even if I fail, god always tell me "I got you"
I was only a cholo-wanna be
but as an smart guy my only choices was to leave
I am Javier G., Jr. with different story
I will be a video game designer and underground rap who don't sleep
I'm almost 18 but still act like an adult when I'm not
I feel scared whenever I think god gonna take my mom
I feel weak every time I woke up
but we all know we gotta be tough
that what make us strong
I only hope that every I am isn't wrong
I dream the same thing until my life is gone
Boy and girl, I am Javier G., Jr.

Missing Feelings

Whenever I sleep, I dream
I flashback, when I think
I sit tight, getting my life right
I feel everything even when I'm holding nothing
When I catch feelings, I can't feel what it really killing
Air is known as Oxygen, I 1st breath when my mom told me "I got you in"
meaning she gave me birth, she the only person I grew up with her
I make sound mute, would've been deaf if no one knew
My heart fall apart like when space cause a shooting star
Shooting across the pretty dark sky, just like I think about my mom in my mind
I swim in pool, hoping devil doesn't take me to hell b'cuz I broke too many rule
Young vision is standing behind me, Ain't for sure if Jesus standing beside me
I cross the dream after looking both ways, but get feelings like I'm get ran over like a pro way
I fall asleep in class, cuz devil putting my asleep while he's about to laugh
an angel fight off to save me from my sleep to death, but I always welcome an angel as a quest
I wake up in the morning thinking what's gonna happen next
For some reasons, I can't fall in love
Can't fall for girl cuz they know what's sup
I feel myself dying, hurting, showing, and sometime giving up
I wake up not wanting to go to school but I only got 1 year left
I'm so close to be 18 so I needa make my behavior to the best.

Kenzik D.
Age 13, Concord

My Favorite Teacher

My favorite teacher Mrs. Wray
was my favorite teacher cause of how
fun she was. She had a project
where we read the book *A Wrinkle
in Time* and after we were done
we watched the movie. She was my
homeroom teacher and I had two
classes with her a day. Later in
the year she told the class
some interesting news. She was
pregnant with a baby girl and was
about to move. Her husband was
in the Navy and got reassigned
so she had to move to Pennsylvania
by May 29th. The class was sad
and some people began to cry. Mrs. Wray
has taught me a lot of things. She was
the best teacher I ever had and
if I can see her again I would
thank her for being a great person
to know.

Beach Days

I remember being at the
beach. I heard seagulls, water splashing,
and kids screaming. I loved the smell
of the taco truck in the parking lot
as a concession stand made hot dogs and
burgers. Eagles flying and diving into
the ocean while dogs bark at
them. I stayed in a motel with
my dad and we watched Friday After
Next cause it was close to Christmas.
We bought some McDonald's
and ice cream. I had a cheeseburger,
fries, and a Gatorade I got from
the gas station. I loved my trip
to Florida and I hope I can do it again.

Mussel

It looks like a big
elf ear. Old torn and beat up.
The outside feels like the side of a
brick and the inside feels like a
moist marble. It is mainly found under the sea and contains
shimmering things. It is found on
rocks in sand and at the bottom
of a lake or the ocean. Sometimes
they are found as a whole or
a half—beautiful always. It felt
like I found gold when I
got it for half an eaten ice cream
cone

Sydney B.

Age 10, Saint Florian

Happy Helper!

One day, when I was in 4th grade (I'm going to 5th grade now) my mother came home from work and she asked me "Do you have any homework?" And I said "No." Then my mom looked in my folder and she said, "You haven't done your homework for two weeks," and my mom and I spent the rest of the night doing my two week old homework and I didn't get to go outside either!

The Laughing Project

I'm going to talk about something that made me laugh really hard. So we were inside of my grandma's car and the laughing sounded like people were screaming. It was my cousin DJ he was about to tell a joke and my friend Melody and I started laughing even though he didn't tell the joke yet and then when he told the joke, DJ said, "A little rain doesn't hurt but a lot of rain does hurt." And then we just started cracking up and then DJ tried to tell a joke again and we started laughing and DJ said, "That was the joke, silence!" We all felt very silly to laugh like that. Then when I got home I was in my room and I was watching TV and I randomly started laughing.

Phone on the Loose!

One day I went to my parent's night thing for camp and I took my phone with me to play games and then, Skylar, Jordan, DJ, me, my mom, Miss Jennifer, and Trachelle were there. I still had my phone. When we finished eating, We went home. I put my phone on the counter for one night, next thing you know, it's gone. I have cried every day. My phone is somewhere in the kitchen. If anyone has seen my phone, call 911 or call 852-FIND-MY-PHONE! PLUS I STILL HAVEN'T FOUND IT! Please call one of those numbers. But the good thing is that I have my iPad and iPod. It's an iPhone 4 with a sparkly purple case. I feel sad that I lost my phone. I play plants vs. zombies.

Fredy C.

Age 15, La Plaza

Sharing Crayons

The first journey I took was when I had to go to preschool. I was afraid when my mom told me that I was going to a place where I can learn and play with kids my age. It first sounded fun, so I agreed to go to school. When I arrived at school my mom had to leave me there, I had no problem with that. I wanna be that guy who shares crayons.

In the future I wanna become that one hero that everyone looks up to. There is many challenges that I have to go through.

My mother told me that I have to commit to my education because it affects my future.

Area 51

In Kings Island there is a ride called Area 51. A lot of people see advanced technology during the ride people think it's fake. In reality the equipment there is real, donated from the government. A lot of people feel entertained and I feel like if the stuff that I'm looking is real. There is an Alien's head in a container full of liquid and a weapon shaped like a gun, but this weapon is different than we imagined. The weapon is glowing green and surrounded by red around it.

My theory about it is that the government gave the advanced technology to them because it would distract the people from wondering about the government. Anyways the people reactions are terrified when they encounter the alien's head.

Jackeline M.

Age 15, La Plaza

Commitment

I called myself out on going on runs. Running non-stop and coming home feeling accompanied like I can actually do it. I started when I started soccer. I knew soccer involved a lot of running, so I pushed myself to run. I motivated myself where I am now.

Inspiration from my dad made me start soccer. He played soccer as a teenager so he taught me a lot about soccer. I don't think I would've done it without him or even started soccer. I wasn't actually interested until I tried it for the first time.

I know soccer is a difficult sport. You need to learn a lot. There's been plenty of times when I really felt like giving up because I didn't feel good enough. In one of my games I made a wrong pass. I thought, "How could I do that." It made me mad because I knew how many people were watching and it was embarrassing to me. I felt horrible, maybe to the point of quitting. I have quit soccer for about a year but I'm back at it now. I feel committed now more than ever.

My Sister

She was only a year old
But she left this world not knowing what is was about
How she could grow up
How she could live her future life.
She left this world without knowing a thing
She had no control towards what happened to her
She didn't even know it was happening
All she knew was that it hurt
And that pain was enough to kill her
SHE DIED—RIP—FOR NO REASON
Her name was Brenda. Birthday—4/20

The Beginning of the Future

I see a family rushed into the hospital. They had been in a terrible car accident. I heard horrifying screams as they came in. Sounds of pain I've never heard before. The little girl asking for help. Her skin pale of all the blood loss. Her parents unable to move called for her. "Grace!" "Grace!" I witnessed the fear in their eyes. I rushed to help this family. As a nurse I knew I couldn't do as much as a doctor. But I tried what I was trained for and what I was capable of doing.

Sterling M., Jr.

Age 12, Saint Florian

Best Memories

I remember when the world was at peace
When the earth had set calmly underneath,
My feet. When the sun was lifted high
Next to the big puffy clouds in the deep blue sky.
People's smiles raised hope;
The helpless felt less needy.

I remember when happiness didn't come from
Electronics, the newest clothes, or shoes
People didn't throw beer bottles in our tall grass
No arguments, no fights, no judgment
No disrespect towards anyone.
When fun times didn't come from sitting on the couch
Or watching television shows or from video games.

Adventure came from the outdoors not a simulator.
People talked to one another, face-to-face.
Not over the phone.
When time gave the best of memories
To hold on to
Forever.

I am...

I am Sterling better known
as K the color I best rep
is BLUE from Marilyn Rd. I
go to CFI #27. I prefer
to eat chicken & Waffles. Soccer
my Game. Madea, Rush Hour
are my favorites. Iggy and
Ariana Grande are entertaining to
me. Kings Island, Holiday World.
Say Hey ho & ignoring Everybody
if you ask me personally
this is who I am...

Bike Crash

Once I was riding my bike then suddenly a car appeared on the road. I had to act fast. I rushed to the sidewalk but forgot that the sidewalk was too high to jump onto so I tried to rush it home but the red, 2011 Jeep Cherokee was just too fast. "Beep, beep. Hurry up kid, I've got to go get some gas." My heart was racing. What if he runs out of gas and I'm to blame, what if he gets out of his car and chases after me? I'm not going to take my chances with him. He has a dent on the left side of the car, a massive and unpleasant scar on the right side of his face. He had a gray stripe on sloppy goatee, two fairly bushy eyebrows, a lot of hair, and a name tag that said Dave O. and Foot Locker on the top. Shocked for my life. He HONKED his horn for a long time. Not being aware I ran into a huge pothole, and huge scars ran on my left thigh. Crying, bleeding, and a horrible memory.

Hugo R.

Age 13, La Plaza

I Am…

I am Hugo Perez R.
My name means juice
I am a Mexican, the next generation, a Polly lover, a brown eyed
I wonder why blood tastes bad
I hear people screaming
I see a picture of people talking
I taste tacos
I smell Mexican food
I feel something hard Ooh it's a rock
I want money
I was a young boy that liked Pokémon
I am a person
I will be a soccer player
I pretend to be a warrior
I feel scared when the lights are off when I'm alone in the house in a thunderstorm
I feel weak when I get up in the morning
I feel strong when I push a door
I hope the world is a better place
I dream of monsters trying to spray paint walls
I am Hugo Perez R.

Football to Fútbol

I used to play a lot of football. And a couple people on the team told me, "You're a Mexican." I said, "Yea that's true." Later that night, I was thinking about it and sitting in my fluffy chair and staring into space. I had this feeling that I'd never felt before. It was a happy feeling that I didn't have to do football anymore because I'd accomplished that already. I had a flashback of what my teammates said and I realized I needed to play soccer. I smiled.

I went to an indoor soccer stadium to practice free kicks and I missed every one. My coach came and said, "Why are you missing all these shots," in a confused voice. And I told him, "Because I am practicing my free kicks." I was missing the goals because I was kicking with the tip of my shoes, instead of the top. I was frustrated like a lion who missed his prey. So I said, "I quit. I can't do this." He said, "Yes you can." I asked him how. He said, "Whenever you kick the ball, your mind is focused on the ball, my foot, and the goal." So I kicked the ball his way. I got closer but still didn't make it in. I tried a few more times and kept hitting the top corner. I told him, "It might work," because I got closer. After thirty or forty shots, I made it. And felt happy as a boy who got his favorite toy at the store.

Three major challenges of soccer are learning how to juke so you can do a trick to get away from the enemy, speed, and open-mindedness. I have to stretch and take warm up laps to increase speed. Having an open mind is important so that you can adapt a play on the field. So if one guy is open, you how to change your plan.

The Vipers were bigger and taller than my team the Chivas. When I found out we had to face them, I said, "I hope we win, but I know we are going to lose." We were tired because the Vipers were faster. They were fouling, but the refs didn't call them. We were losing 5 to 4 and some guy got a lucky kick on our team to even up the score 5-5. The refs put in penalty kicks for both teams. Whoever got more goals would win. It was 4 to 4. The Vipers were in the lead and it was up to me tom make the last one. I was scared like being chased by a poisonous snake. I took a deep breath and had a flashback of Coach Juan giving me advice for how to make this goal. I turned back to look at my coach. I looked back at the crowd. And it gave me confidence. I looked at the goal, then the goalie, and thought in my mind as if I were the goalie. I looked at the ball. I put the ball how I wanted it, because Coach Juan said if you put it on the black hexagon, it's good luck. It took a minute to think. In my mind, I took all the shots to find the best plan. I kicked the ball and it curved. The ball made it into the left corner like a mouse going into its hole. The crowd screamed. It sounded like I was in a professional stadium. I felt proud of myself for succeeding. Then I told myself, "Yea. I shouldn't be a football player. I should be a professional Mexican soccer player."

Michael Baumann

Student Teacher, La Plaza and Saint Florian

Trust

Joan Didion in her 2006 collection of nonfiction reminds us that we tell ourselves stories in order to live. Stories help us to remember. They help us to sort, to process, to heal and to deal, to learn, share, and forgive. They help us to breathe.

And this book echoes with stories. Please decant them. They will do you some good. They will help you to live.

Before drinking deeply, though, know that this book didn't—happen—unprovoked. Our authors first recalled, then voiced, then revised, then published—and sometimes performed—their nonfiction, narrative-based memoir writing. Working with these authors for the third summer, I learned more about the messy, the beautifully disastrous, the achingly human, the powerful, the empowering, the therapeutic, and—yeah—the dangerous act of writing. In order to recall, voice, and revise their prose first they needed to trust themselves: I feel a central ingredient in our act of storytelling is trust. Trust between the writer and the reader, trust between the writer and the page, trust between the writer and the self.

Trust between our writers and you. They are trusting you to listen to their stories.

Parker Palmer's *A Courage to Teach: Exploring the Inner Landscape of a Teacher's Life* is a phenomenal text, and if you haven't yet read it, I recommend. Palmer encourages trust and vulnerability as mighty dynamics in the classroom, suggesting that, when we ask students to occupy the vulnerable space of writing, we ask them to compose with their authentic voices; what then, Palmer asks, could eclipse the necessity of trust? He says, "Teaching, like any truly human activity, emerges from one's inwardness, for better or worse. As I teach, I project the condition of my soul onto my students, my subject, and our way of being together." And so I have learned to fold such dynamics into my own teaching philosophy and identity.

An aspirant composition instructor, though, I hope that the moments during which I tasted trust this summer will burgeon into a rich bank of experience. The Indiana Writers Center's Build a Rainbow summer program has provided just such a burgeoning for me: over the past three summers (if my calculations are precise) I have enjoyed 141 hours working with our authors at the three sites we workshop. That's about 0.0007% of my life.

So clearly I have a lot left to learn. But I can already count a great deal of experiences involving trust.

As you read this book abundant with stories, please remember Joan Didion's words—that these stories help us to live—and please elect to recall some of your own. Then—trust your readers, trust your pages, trust yourself.

Write.

Wesley G.

Age 11, Saint Florian

Gran Jan

My Gran Jan died by getting hit by a bus, but she was on her way home. The bus crashed into her by running a red light and the sad thing is she died on my birthday. I was turning 5. My favorite thing about her was that she would buy me anything I wanted but I never used her. She was a great great Gran Jan. When my mom found out she started to be sad and she cried and she was sad. But it's okay because she is in the heavens with the Lord. I felt happy when she passed 'cause she's in a better place. But I will cherish and love her forever.

If I could tell her anything I would tell her I love her.

The End

My Apartment

One time me and my mom lived in these other apartments for six years and we always got free cable because we live in the last town house and we always walked to Walgreens to buy some candy to eat with the movies.

When we first moved there I was a baby. But our 6th year I was six years old. Then finally when I turned seven we moved. Now me and my mom are living in a different apartments called Woodlake.

This time I'm not a baby, I'm going to 6th grade. I'm going to Westlane Middle School this year. But I'm so excited because this is my first year having a locker.

I am excited to have a locker because I like the way the door opens. My locker is going to be a private locker.

It's going to be private because I don't want people going into it. And they have better lunch.

Helping My Family

One time I went to my granny's house and we went to Walmart to get some groceries and she had gotten a lot of groceries. We went home and had gotten milk, Cheez-Its, goldfish, chicken, and steak. She was bringing them in and she asked me why am I not helping and I said I don't know. She got mad and told me that I need to help her. I went to help and I saw she got my favorites pack, twizzlers. But she said I have to leave her alone because she has to study for her test. It was a state test that she studied for all week and I helped her around the house. But most of the time I watched TV. And she has a dog Penny who is scared of everything. But movement is mostly what she's scared of and sometimes when she sees people she does not know she screams and scratches. But when she gets to know you she's nice. But when I jump at her she does not get scared. I love her. And guess what, my granny passed the test. She called and told everyone about it and she called my mom and told her. My mom was all happy too but we celebrated and made a cake. She put icing on the cake and it was my favorite, caramel! It was white cake and it had Brown cake bread sealed up. The next time we went to the store she did not have to even tell me I just did it. She was always wanting me to help and she likes for me to open the door for her and my mother but I just do it all the time.

My mom sometimes makes me do the chores but I try to get out of doing them. Sometimes my dad just helps my mom but I take the groceries in the house. I also help her wash clothes but my dad doesn't. He makes me do them. But my mom said that she wants him to help sometimes but he does when she asks him to. But I just love helping my grandma because it was just something about her that makes me help her. But sometimes I just don't help. Mom said that she loves me helping my granny but sometimes I love helping for no reason. I love going to my granny's house. She picks me up from camp all the time but she didn't this week because she's out of town.

Trinity C.

Age 12, Saint Florian

Dance with my Father

It was a warm dark school night and my school was having a father daughter dance. When we walked in the cafeteria there was lots and lots of decoration, loud music, and lots of food and dessert. After I had my food I went in the gym and danced with some of my friends. After a few minutes dancing with my friends the D.J. told everybody to go get their dads because the D.J. was going to play a slow song. After the two minute slow song the D.J. played some upbeat music. After a long time of dancing I went to go get a dessert. It was almost time to go but before we left the D.J. played one more slow song, so everybody got on the gym floor and everybody started slow dancing. While we were slow dancing my dad started singing and a couple of people started looking at us. I was so embarrassed and didn't want to go to another father daughter dance ever. The End.

The Non-Stop laugher

On a Friday afternoon my loving care group got split up because my care givers boss wasn't there so she had to take over while she was gone. So I had to go to the first grade group with my friends Nolan, London, and Simone. When everybody put their stuff in a basket and got seated....everybody had a snack, after snack all of the groups got lined up to go to the next activity. My group was lining up to go to the computer lab and while we were waiting my friend Nolan told me something so funny but I forgot what he said, but when he told me I just couldn't stop laughing and as I was continuously laughing I ended up peeing on myself. When I was laughing so hard everybody was staring at me like I was crazy freak show. When I was laughing I could not breathe at all 'cause it was just that funny.

The End!

Death of a Neighbor

It was on a dark and windy school night and me, my brother, my sister, and my mom were on our way back home. As we were getting closer to the house we all heard sirens, but in my mind I thought that there was a fire truck or police car driving behind us. But it turned out the police car and fire truck was in our neighborhood. Me and my mom were trying to figure out why they were here, but me and my mom thought our house was on fire but it wasn't. When we drove in the area we saw two fire trucks and a police car by our next door neighbor's house. When we drove down to our house my mom tried to drive up in our driveway but we couldn't because there was a fire truck in the way, so my mom had to figure something else to try to get in our driveway. So my mom told my brother, my sister, and I to get out the car and go into the house and start our homework. It was so hard to do our homework because the sirens were loud and annoying. So we were waiting on my mom to get in the house but she was outside asking our neighbor across the street about what happened and he was like I'm not really sure what happen. After that happened, the fire truck finally moved out of my mom's way. So my mom drove the car in the garage. So my brother and sister and I tried to do our homework and my mom was trying to figure out what was for dinner. Time was ticking by and my dad made it home. When he got in the door he told us about what happen next door. My dad said, "So our neighbor said that my wife was getting ready to walk out the room when we trip over the dog and hit her head really hard on the dresser and fell and was died." My mom was so amazed and puzzled. After that whole tragedy the two fire trucks left. After they left the FBI came to investigate the house for evidence. The stayed all night and it probably took them forever to get all the evidence. After a whole hour they finally left.

Morgan L.

Age 13, Concord

The Spoon

I am a spoon I'm woody and
splintery. I can make soup. I'm used
to spank. I can stir paint. I can
be different sizes. We can be
made out of metal, plastic,
or wood. I can help you make ice cream
juice and lemonade. I'm a spoon
so don't get spanked. I can make
different soups like tomato, chili pepper,
broccoli. I stir paint with water
and mod podge to give a glossy
finish. I'm a beautiful thing so use
me right. I can also make pretzels
so yummy and good mmmm
so yummy. I am a spoon.
I'm a multi-purpose.

The Sister

My little sister grabbed my
Doll's hair and slowly pulled
it back. "That's perfect," I said.
She said, "Now you try."
I slowly pulled it back.
Then I pulled it back with
a rubber band tying it tight up. "Yay,"
I said, "I did it." Thanks to my
sister I learned how to do hair.
~For Abigail

A Small Forest

When I walk down your path
I see pretty things.

Your plants all so nice. When I
see your water so clear and sometimes
mucky like Bread when it's good and bad.

When I saw the dew on some of
the plants they shine bright like a diamond.

When it's quiet I hear the
chirps of bird. I can also hear
the flowing water so slow and quiet.

When I felt the mint leaf
and I smelled it. it remind me of
a york peppermint patty.

This forest so small but beautiful
and full of life.

Mary Redman

Volunteer, Concord

As a high school English teacher, I always knew the importance of sharing models of writing with students. I thought it was important for students to see me tackle assignments I gave them, so I was really pleased that Shari thought it was important for all of us, teacher, interns, and volunteers to contribute our own writing to the examples she shared with our students at Concord. It took me a while to find the time and inspiration to write a poem to share with our kids, but I did so last week during our fieldtrip to the Marian University Eco Lab. Because the prompt was one that asked us to write a poem inspired by a walk in nature, I wrote about my dog, Enzo. The kids listened politely as I read:

Walk With Enzo

Enzo moves close to be collared. A leash is his *call*
of the wild. We walk…
then pause, as his part-pug nose pushes
into a cast-off McDonald's bag, streaked with ketchup.

Under a line of crowded pines, he sniffs
a soggy cottonwood seed, fluff flattened to pavement by rain, no way
for a tree to grow. Instinct makes him mark the spot, perhaps a show of
dominance. He jerks the leash in my hand; a futile race begins

and ends , as his bushy-tailed foe, too quick to catch, gloats
in victory from a locust branch,.
No matter—a new interest—goose droppings, green and moist, attract
his notice next.
Jaws clamp around a morsel, and he eyes me, expectantly.

Will I compete for the glob in his mouth? He can't conceive I have
no appetite for such delicacies.
One more stop, a spot he chooses with care: a slow squat with his
back to me.
Hind legs respond to an inborn command, kicking dirt and loose grass
to bury what he's left.

I lean down, bag his leavings, and we turn together for home.
Hot and tired from our outing, Enzo sprawls on cool kitchen tiles.
A weary tourist in the wild, he has struck a good bargain being mine:
yielding the appeals of nature for the comforts of domesticity.

When I finished reading, our students were appreciative of my poem, and one girl asked, "Miss Mary, did you name your dog Enzo after the dog in *The Art of Racing in the Rain*? I was pleased to tell her that that was exactly where my Enzo got his name. I was also pleased to feel like a full-fledged member of our writing community, who shares not only an enthusiasm for writing with my kids at Concord, but also a love for some of the same books.

Roman D.

Age 10, Saint Florian

Totino's Pizza: Triple Cheese

One day, my mom and I went to Walmart and my mom went into the frozen pizza aisle. She grabbed three Totino's Pizza: Combination and said, "Which one do you want? Sausage, Pepperoni, or Combination?" Instead I chose a different pizza and pointed to Triple Cheese. She said, "Which one?" and I said, "That one, Triple Cheese," and my mom grabbed four of 'em and we were out of the store.

That night we had the pizzas for dinner and she said they took thirty minutes to cook. So I went back, played the game. Before I could even win my mom yelled, "Dinner's ready!" I already knew that meant to get my dad and tell him he needs to come down to eat.

When I took my first bite of Triple Cheese I fell into Triple Cheese heaven the sun became a Triple Cheese pizza and the sky turned yellow. I devoured the whole pizza in 5 minutes and took the second pizza too.

The Order: 1886

The order of 1886 was a prank against American soil. Russia, Japan, and Germany were creating giant water balloons. On, January 27th, 1886 The Order was given to fire at American Soil. The huge balloon dropped and it exploded with water on New Mexico and Arizona. The Grand Canyon became a lake. Then, Albert Einstein discovered the splitting of water Atom. We made five water Atoms and fired them back. We made mega floods and we won the prank war.

Avenger Car Crash

We got in my mom's Dodge Avenger to go to my grandmother's birthday party, and by the time we got out of the garage I was out cold. My seat belt wasn't buckled because I was way too tired to use it. All I saw was darkness. My dad allowed the van to turn and then we followed right behind them. That's when a car hit us and I woke up partially. I was shaking around in the car. I became half-asleep but woke up. Our car fell into a ditch. My leg felt broken and I barely climbed out the car. I was crying. The ambulance took me in. I was going like 100 mph and I was hyperventilating, but I took deep breaths and got through. It turned out that I had a bone bruise on my leg and had to be escorted out of the hospital.

The Claw

I had just finished dinner when I was going to the couch. I was about 6 years old at the time and my dad was on the couch. He was watching some Drama show with my mom and that's when it happened. That's when the claw hit me! My dad grabbed my leg and squeezed it. I started cracking up and I tried to escape the claw and take my dad's hand off me. Instead I fell off the couch. I couldn't catch my breath and my face became red. That's when I banged my head on the table and was about to cry when I rubbed it and just started laughing again.

Quanell C.

Age 6, Saint Florian

A Good Day

One time me and my mom were exercising on TV tonight and my brother jumped on my mom and fell between my mom's legs, and that made me laugh. We tried to do pushups. We had to do 100 of them. My arms hurt. We got tired. We fell asleep. We woke up in the morning and decided to exercise some more. I got a six pack. My auntie came over. I asked her, "Do you have a six pack?" She said, "No I have a seven pack." On TV the cat chased the mouse. The mouse's body stretched out and the cat chased him into a diaper. It was Tom and Jerry.

My Cleats

My Cleats are for playing soccer. They are blue. First I slide my feet in and then tie them. They feel a lot like regular shoes other than the little bumps on the bottom. We take out the soccer ball and then someone comes to kick it. I try to take the ball from the other team but the other team keeps scoring goals. My team scored more points and finally won the game.

When My Mom Tricked Me

When I was watching TV my mom said there was a pillow behind me and there wasn't. Then she said a lamp was falling on me and there wasn't. She tried to trick me and said my bed was gone but it wasn't. Then I laughed!

My Scar

The scar is on my ankle, because I broke it and fell off my bike at my grandma's. My mom helped me. It was bleeding. My Grandma put tissue on it. It was my right ankle. We went to the doctor. First they put tissue on it then they put a cast on it. My cast was red. I got to pick the color. I got to put stickers on it, too. They were Toy Story. I like Toy Story. My favorite character is Buzz. When I went to school all the people signed it with markers. The cast felt weird when I took a bath.

Da'Laysia G.

Age 6, Saint Florian

Cinnamon Toast

One time I got bit by a little puppy then I was bleedin' then I got a bandage she was a girl and named Cinnamon and her last name was Toast. She was soft. She is a good girl. This happened in self-defense. My mommy helped me get a bandage and my mommy gave her a toy. Her first name was sweet and her last name was sweet. Cinnamon is brown and her ears look like wolves' ears. She puts her ears down when people are yelling at each other. Her tail looks like a fox.

Playing with Cinnamon Toast

You eat cinnamon toast but you don't eat the dog, and I have sunflowers, and they are white and yellow inside. My dog is named Cinnamon Toast. She is a Chihuahua and she is a girl.

One day I was playing with her bone and I throw it at her. She caught it with her mouth. She's a good catcher. She is a good dog, but she bites. She drinks her water and eats her food. It was when I was at home. I love her.

My Two Scars

One time I got two scars-one on my waist and on my leg at the same time. I was playing with my dogs. I was in the kitchen with my dog, Cinnamon Toast, a sweet dog. I went to wash my hand before I ate dinner. We bought dinner at the Chinese place. The Chinese place is real nice—I like their rice. You can have breakfast there! Then we started to eat, but we said our prayer before that. That morning after we ate, my mommy said it was time to go to bed. 8, 9, 10 o'clock. Then I had a dream about a shark. He was trying to bite me. I was trying to swim fast and I couldn't. When I got out of the water the shark was dead. He had blood. Then after that I went back home In the dream I have magic. When I woke up I had two scars.

Jasmine T.

Age 10, Saint Florian

Surprise Apology

I remember the time I hurt my Aunt's feelings. It was April 1st the day before her birthday. She was cooking dinner In the kitchen. She was cooking Chicken with corn and Green beans. It took an hour to Get everything prepared. My mom was helping each other out. My Aunt always cooks the chicken. The chicken was good but when she made it that day it tasted kinda funny. Maybe she put too much seasoning on the chicken. Maybe I already had a Bad taste in my mouth. I was really scared to tell her that the chicken was not so tasty but I told her anyway but then when I threw it away she started crying. *Splash*. A soggy tear came down from her eye to her cheek. My mom ran and got my Aunt a tissue and wiped her cheeks and eyes.

I was sad that I had made my Aunt cry. So I wanted to do something special for her so I got some of my cousin's to help me plan her birthday party. I got my cousin Jakalayah and my other cousin Britteny and we went to the store. My mom drove us and we Got some streamers and balloons and some white ribbons. I want to do the part at her house. So my cousin Jakalayah took her to the mall. While they were there out shopping me and my cousin started put up the decorations for the party. When it was 4:00 there was 10 minutes Left. They said they were going to come back at 4:10 to 5:10. We ordered some Food and everybody was wearing white and black. We started to find places to hide. It was 4:09—one minute till they got here. When they walked in, we all jumped out and yelled "Surprise!" She was so shocked. She came over and Gave me a hug and said, "I Love you."

What I Did for the Very First Time

What I did for the very first time was go swimming. The first time I went swimming I was 6 years old. We went to the YMCA. My mom held me in her hands and carried me in the water and she put me in the water by 1 and 2 feet and she put me by the playground area. I went down the slide and the slide takes you under water and when you come out, you are still under water.

Then I came up from the water and I swam to my mom for the first time. She was so proud of me so she carried me to the 3 to 4 feet and I was ok. The 4 to 5 feet and I was pretty OK. I was ok because my mom was right behind me and if I started to drown, my mom would come and save me.

My mom carried me on her back to the Deep End. She went to 7 and 8 feet. That was the deepest end of the pool. There was barely any people in 8 feet. The water touched my mom's neck 'cause she is really tall. When we were getting ready to leave, she told me to put my towel down. When we were loading the car up, she put me in the back seat and fastened my seatbelt. She told me to Dry Off while we were heading home.

When we got home my Dad asked how I did and I said, "Mommy took me to 8 feet," and then he said he was so proud of me. So the next time I go swimming, I will remember what my dad told me (never be afraid of water). And from that day on, I was never afraid of the water. So the next day we went, my mom sat on the beach chair and watched me. So when we were about to leave my mom said we can stay for another 10 minutes. She was ready to go but I wasn't ready. So when we left my mom said, "Let's go get something to eat."

Jaquayla J.

Age 7, Saint Florian

I Remember My Mom, Jericha

I remember when I lost my mother. It was a Friday. My mother was cleaning up at night. Then I went to sleep. She came in the bed and she said I can play on her phone. In the morning, Tia, her friend, was trying to wake her up. She is her friend who spent the night. She couldn't wake her up. My mom died. I was six. Then I missed school and she missed work. I was very sad because I was scared of the dark. At the funeral I was acting like I was sleep, because I didn't want to cry. I loved my mother and I miss her a lot. After she died, I went to live with my godmother Courtney and then grandmommy and now I live with my grandmom. I miss my mom. I remember when she was at my birthday and we went to Chuck E Cheese. And I love Barbies and she gave me a really, really pretty Barbie. She was a Black Barbie with a ponytail and a half pink and half purple dress. I remember when on Halloween she gave me some high heels that looked like hers and I dressed up like a half devil/half angel. If I could talk to my mom I would tell her I miss her a lot.

JAQUAULA

J = Johnson
a = Apple
Q = Quiet
u = upset
a = ape
y = yes
l = little
a = awesome

Girls Like Heels

I wear pink heels when we go to church. Girls like wedge heels.
I wear them with a skirt that's pink with a red heart and a pink shirt that has an "M" on it. The "M" shows that I have a mom.
I got my shoes from the mall.
They're the very cutest ever in the whole wide world.

Serenity N.

Age 8, Saint Florian

Grandma Died

One day my grandma and my cousin David was going to church. David said, "Come on" but my grandma said, "No you go and I will be there." David said, "Where is she?" Then he went back home. He knocked on my grandma's door. He went inside the room. She was lying on the floor. Her heart stopped and she was dead and I was very sad. My mom told me that my Grandma died it was during 2000 and I was born in 2005.

J's on My Feet

My J's are blue and black. I wear my J's all the time. My favorite place to wear them is the skating rink. When I go there, I was walking around the skating rink. Then I went home. Then the next day I went to my dad's house and my dad has J's too and my sister. But his J's are blue and my sister has blue and gray.

Getting Hurt

I remember when I fell. Then my whole knee was bleeding all down my leg. I was playing with my sister in the yard at our old house. We were playing tag, and I was *it*. Then I chased my sister on the patio. Then I trip and fell on the concrete. Then Bugs were surrounding me. Then I had to go in the house and my mom put a bandage on it. But it hurt.

My First Time at a Grave

I remember when I went to a grave with my Aunt Penny, my cousins, my brother, and my sister. It was in Michigan. Then my cousin was crying at the wrong grave. Then we took pictures with my family and my grandmother.

Patricia Cupp
Volunteer, Concord

Child in the Barn

She holds the baby chicks, hands curving
to nest. She touches one with her chin,
careful in a way I have never seen before.
In the barn full of animals, the donkey, the lamb,
the calf and the goat, she returns only to the chicks,
this girl of three, who ran to me this morning,
come quick, something has happened,
meaning petals had fallen from the roses.
Her thin shoulder against me, her hair
dark with sweat, she shines in the barn's dust,
this quiet girl who wishes on stars
and is responsible for everything.

"Everyone you will ever meet knows something you don't."
Bill Nye the Science Guy

I would add to that: "Especially children."

Counselor Niki

Saint Florian

My Best Friend Cousin

We've been friends since day one
We were two years apart and had so much fun
We were great friends you and me
Just the way family is supposed to be
Whenever we were together you couldn't shut us up
And that would make our parents fuss
But after a while they realized it wasn't going to stop
We were just THAT close
We got into so much stuff you and me
My brother and Brianna to complete the crew
We were the four musketeers
Always together, we knew each others fears
You were my first best friend that wasn't my brother
And I wouldn't ask for any other
I loved you through the good and the bad
I'll always remember the fun times that we had
The late nights and sleepovers that we had
Our favorite episode of avatar that made us laugh
And gave us the phrase "Let Us Leave, Lettuce leaf"
It will always make me laugh, smile and think of you
I'm sad that you're gone but I do believe
That you are in a better place and at peace
You knew that I love you I was sure of that
Best friends to the end, always had your back
My best friend cousin, that was you
My best friend cousin, I will miss you

Rafael S.

Age 12, Saint Florian

The Very Sad Day

When I was in 5th grade, 11 years old, the school day ended. A few hours ago I got News. Some very sad News. My Mom told me my grandpa got cancer and we had to go to Iowa to help around the house and be with my grandpa. So we packed up and hit the road. When we finally got there my Mom dropped us off at our cousin's house. We stayed overnight a couple days, but we heard grandpa went to the hospice. We went to the hospice every day to visit, but one night it was his time, so a priest came in and said some stuff, and grandpa said, "I am going to see the Lord do not be sad." But of course everyone wept and wept the whole night.

I Remember

I remember my favorite book.
I remember that I am hungry.
I remember my name.
I remember that I have 2 dogs.
I remember I like shooting games.
I remember that I want Xbox Live.
I remember that I have 2 cats.
I remember my last name.
I remember that I am thirsty.
I remember my favorite animal.
I remember I am half Mayan.

Collaborative Poem

Concord

The Concord Poets

Make us out of our imagination:
Lucky charms, Christmas bells,
papier mâché and piano keys,
glass masquerade masks,
cotton candy people,
globes of the earth,
and little light-up rings.
Silver spoons, bongos,
rain sticks.
String us together with
pretzel knots and tater tots,
shoe knots and fisherman knots.
Hang us on your sycamore tree
or on your front porch.
When the wind blows
we will rock,
and talk,
and play,
and sing
our song, a perfect tune.

Jalen K.

Age 8, Saint Florian

Bike Wreck

I remember when I was riding my bike really fast down the street. It was Saturday. It was summer. I tried to ride with one hand. Then I ran over a rock and a piece of tree. Then I fell off my Bike. And my Bike was still going with no one on it. Then I started to Bleed on my leg. When my Bike got to the other house it fell. My Bike it was yellow and black, and as tall as a table.

Drive-In Seat Pranks

I was at a drive-in. I pulled a prank on my brother, Jeremiah. I had a big water bottle. It is a big fat water bottle, and it was 6 inches. I poured the water on his chair. He sat in it. And it made a sound. Then he said, "I peed my pants." Then he went to go get a napkin. He dried his seat off. Then he went to go throw the napkins away and while he went to the dumpster I had went in the car and got some glue. I put glue on his chair. He came back to sit in it. When the movie was over he had tried to get up, then when he got up the chair was stuck to him.

My Neighborhood

I live in Apartments. And the name is Country Lake. I live in the front of the apartments. They are red bricks. I have friends that live on each side of my house. Security and policemans always come 5 hours every day because my apartments is a bad apartments—like people always get in fights. And kids always cussing. Every time I come outside there are a lot of kids riding their bikes really fast. And there's this one big ole field as big as a football field and we play football and soccer there. Sometimes we be racing and next to it is a playground, but it's all torn apart and stuff. Next to my apartments is my cousin Elyjah's apartments. In their apartments, their park is way better than mine. So I go play over there. It's a fun playground.

William R. II

Age 7, Saint Florian

Blue Drumstick Love

The first time I ever played the drums I was three years old. It was a black drums, not the kind from Christmas. My dad gave it to me but it broke. It was an electric drum set and I wore headphones because my mother said it was too loud. She still hates me for that. Now I can play the church's drums. They were gray or blue—a little bit of blue and a little bit of gray. It sounds like "*Pah, tss, pah pah tss. pah, tss, pah pah tss.*" The sanctuary has a keyboard. My little brother plays the keyboard. Walter's five and I'm five. We play gospel because it's a church. Blue drumstick love. I love my blue drumstick.

Dogs at My House

I have dogs at my house. The girl is Unique. The boy's name is Pongo. Another girl one is Simone. Another boy one is Sonya. Simone bites my toes a lot. Unique likes to sit around and Sonya watches TV with me. Sonya just turned 6. Simone just turned 18. Unique likes me. She licks me a lot. I show her some tricks, like roll over on me.

The Water Slide and the Song

Mom helped me at the water slide. It was at the gym. I was a lot of scared. My daddy was with us and he didn't almost die from water splashing. He splashed water on me. My mom helped me because I was scared because I thought Daddy was going to get hurt. I'm still going to be scared. I'm scared of the dark. My mom sang me a song. I sang happy.

Twenty-Four Cheeseburgers

My favorite food is a cheeseburger. I make them with my mom, dad, and baby sister. I put lettuce, ketchup, cheese, and mustard on a bun. When we make them, it takes some time. We make french-fries and a banana smoothie to go along with them. Sometimes we make gooey, gooey watermelon smoothies. I would like to eat 24 cheeseburgers.

Stephanie M.

Age 12, Saint Florian

I Remember When My Brother Was Born

When my brother was born it started the day before. That Sunday I went home with my aunt and she took me to the hospital. We took blankets and pillows for me and my cousin. When we got to the hospital me and my cousin put two chairs together and took our blankets out and then went into my mom's room to see how she was doing. She told me that nothing would be happening for a long time so me and my cousin went back to the lobby. Then my other aunt came and we just relaxed for the night. At about 12:30 my aunt and my cousin went back to their house and although I didn't want to (I wanted to stay with my mom) I went home with them and hung out. The next morning we went back and did the same thing. At about lunchtime my dad bought us some pizza. At 3:15 my mom texted me and told me she was about to start pushing. I had thought I would be really nervous but I was actually calm. At 3:30 my baby brother was born. Once they told me she was all cleaned off I got to go in and hold him. I was really happy that he was finally here.

The First Time I Held My Brother

The first time I held my brother was life changing. I had just received a text saying that my brother was born. All I could think about was what he looked like and when I was going to hold him. Finally my dad came out and told me that I could come back into the room. I practically ran back to her room. When I got into the room he had just been cleaned off. My mom and dad had already held him and now it was my turn. My mom handed the baby to my dad and handed him to me once I had sat down. I had a mix of emotions. I was happy and excited he was here. I was wondering what he would look like and if I would be able to see him first crawl and walk. I was also almost sad because I was an only child for 10 years and now I had a baby brother, but I didn't really worry about that. All I was really thinking about was how happy I was to finally hold my brother.

When the World Stopped

I was 5 years old. We were running from the tagger. I turned around to see where she was. I was ok for now, but since I was running with 6, 7, & 8 year olds I had to run as fast as I could to get to base because I was afraid if I was tagged I would be *it* forever. As I turned back around I found myself colliding with another girl. She had accidently tripped me. I fell & scraped my cheek on the blacktop. I laid there while it seemed the whole world stopped around me. Everyone stopped running while my aunt ran to pick me up. She ran me in the building. At first I didn't cry because I was in shock. Once I was in the building I had started to cry. I started to look around. I looked at my aunt's jacket. It was stained red from my cheek. My cousin helped keep me calm. After a while I joined the kids. My parents told me not to run but I found a loophole, speed walking & jogging. All in all I was ok.

Marcel A.

Age 13, Concord

My Monument

I want them to make a monument of me.
I want it to be big like Mount Rushmore
and made of metal and diamonds.
I want a big stack of video games next to me.
I want it to be painted.
I want the paint to be brown and metallic colors.

I want my family to be right next to me
because they're a part of my life.
We're all standing normally like we always do—
my mom, dad, my stepdad and stepmom, and my sister and brother.

I want people to think, "He was a nice man"
and think my family was the best family they could be.

My monument says:
To have a better life pray for each other.

New York

My favorite place is my home because
I get to see my dog. My favorite
country is New York it is my dream
to go to New York. It's one of the
safest places to be at as you can
hide in the laboratory that you built.
I probably want to be a spy.
At least I will have a home for
the rest of my life.

The Woods

There are strange animals. There are
animals in the pond that are
weird. There was trees blowing, people
talking, and birds chirping. I can't
figure what they are saying.
I wonder if talking about me?
Birds, fly and chirp, a deer jumps.
It's strange that they can talk to each other
without us knowing.
The deer make a creepy noise. They sneak up on you.
The snakes hiss and the
flowers move.

Jaime J.

Age 11, Saint Florian

My BFF Kayla

I remember a time I laughed so hard that my stomach started hurting. One day me and my BFF Kayla were having a sleep over. When she came there was a spark on my face. Then I gave her a big hug. The first thing we did was play the Wii. I kept beating her because I've played all of them before and mastered them. Then we played Just Dance 2014. Kayla was not very good. But it was all ok. Because she beat me. Even though she dances like a penguin in lava we still had fun. Then we watched some movies and went to bed. The next day we woke up at about 9:00 AM and got ready to go to Sky Zone. When we came back we went in my backyard to play on my swing set. Even though it was old and rusty. She sat on the baby swing and I started pushing her then she started making baby noises. It was so funny that I threw up the cheese pizza that we had just eaten. I looked like cat food with rotten Cheetos. Then she stepped in it, slipped, and fell. I laughed so hard. We still laugh about it to this day.

Land of Happiness

Kindergarten was up next ready to take me in after leaving Day Care. I was really worried about Kindergarten. I was scared that the teacher was going to be mean and rude. And that I would have no friends. And I knew that without a doubt it would happen. And there it was, the first day of Kindergarten. My mom walked in with me. I was behind her as if no one could see me. Then we got closer and closer to the door. Then I thought, "Aww, man I entered the death room." But once I had come out from behind my mom, the teacher had the biggest smile on her face. And the first words she said was, "Hi Jaime. Welcome to my classroom. My name is Mrs. L., let me show you around." And immediately I thought, "Wow, I love my teacher already." And the room was amazing. It looked like a land of happiness. And it smelled like vanilla. Ever since I've been in her class she always said I was here favorite. And I never knew why. And 2 years later I visited her and she had the biggest smile just like in Kindergarten. And memories strolled back.

Cheeseburger

Smack! down the patties go, on the oil covered pan. Sizzling as the patty settles in the bubbly oil. Chopping the tomatoes and the onions, pulling the fresh and leafy green lettuce, washing them with cold water. Flipping the patty on the other side with a powerful sizzle. "Almost done," said my dad. Unwrapping the American cheese, putting it on the patty as the cheese melts. Getting the soft buns, meat first, tomatoes, onion, lettuce, ketchup makes the perfect juicy burger on a hot July day.

Diabetic Salt

My sister is always the one who my parents tell stories about because most of the dumb stuff always happens to her. And when I mean dumb I mean the things she says is dumb. Every year my family and I go to the fair. But there is this one stand that we go to no matter what. It's a place where you can get corn on the cob and frozen apple cider. My sister and my dad get the corn, but me and my mom get the apple cider. So we had just got back from getting on the rides and we were about to go. But Lorin wanted to get some corn along with my dad. They gave my sister her corn and they had a station where you can put seasoning on your corn. So my sister walked up to the stand and she puts a lot of salt and her corn and says, "Wow, I'm going to have diabetes." And my mom said, "Lorin, that's for sugar." And we started laughing. She felt so dumb. She was so embarrassed.

Skylar B.

Age 8, Saint Florian

The Circus Accident

Me and my family where going to the car and my dad had a race to see who could get to the car first. So we ran to the car. Then, I tried to go over a pothole! So, then I fell and skid on the concrete! So now I have three scars on my knee.

Humungus Gungus Wave

I remember going to Pensacola, Florida and trying to surf my first wave on my boogie board. Well...It didn't go so well. So I had already got on my boogie board. And then a-PAUSE: *what am I supposed to say again? "Whisper. whisper. whisper"...oh yeah!* PLAY:
HUMUNGUS
GUNGUS
WAVE!
So then I got on the wave. And then my sister said: "No! You're gonna fall—SPLOOSH—off." *Applause.* Well how was I supposed to know better? And then later we were telling mom to get in the water. And she was sitting in the water. It was blue, warm, and salty. Mom sat in the water and we yelled, "Wave! Wave! Wave!" She waved at us, because she didn't know we were talking about the ocean. She screamed and *sploosh*! She was dunked by the wave!

The Mayo Situation

One day my sister was teasing me. So I got the can of Mayo and I had a butter knife so I could play a prank on my sister. After that I snuck in my sister's room and then I found her backpack and her underwear and I spread the mayo in her backpack and underwear. I did it after I got home from school. I did it because I was mad that she was teasing me about still playing with dolls. She opened her backpack to get a pencil and saw the mayo there. The next day when she was getting a pair of underwear she discovered the other mayo. And She screamed, "Mommy! Skylar put mayo in my stuff!" After that, we had a discussion and I was grounded for a week.

THE END

The Rainy Day

One day it was rainy. So I asked my dad if I could go outside to run in the rain with my sister and my cousin. And he said yes! When we got out of the garage it was cold, and wet. We stepped in lots of puddles and raced across the street.

Sevan W.

Age 6, Saint Florian

Phony

I remember William called me phony and he made me mad. Phony means I have fake hair. I looked at him when I was mad, and I told my teacher Mrs. W. It happened today in art class when I was done with my snake. He was calling my hair fake. I didn't call him a name back. I just told the teacher.

A Fun Day

I remember the day I went to Chuck E. Cheese and the park and Sky Zone and Monkey Joe's and the library. I got in the ball pool and I got under the balls and nobody could see me. At the park I went on the slide, the swing, the monkey bars and an up-through-down thing. I rode a horsie. His name was Charles. At Sky Zone, I got 5 prizes. I did a backflip on the trampoline. I saw a big monkey at Monkey Joe's It was real. It fed me a banana, but I was supposed to feed him. It was super weird, I don't even like bananas. I read books at the library. I sat on a turtle chair and watched the TV. The book popped up and somebody on the TV read it to me. It was a wonderful fun day and I had fun.

Cowgirl Boots

I have a pair of pink and purple cowgirl boots and I wore them over my dad's. My dad said, "They're pretty." Then we went to the mall. Then I got outfits. Then I bought some sparkly shoes. Then I screamed so loud everybody left the store and I was the only one there, and I enjoyed myself. I wore those boots when I was at the roller cave skating rink. They let me buy a colorful shirt and a glow in the dark bracelet and a glow in the dark necklace.

The Neighborhood and the Ice Cream Man

One day me and my daddy and my mommy and little sister Tsion went to the ice cream man. I had 30 bucks so I could get three things. The first I got was my bubblegum Hello Kitty Ice cream. The next one I got was a vanilla w/ chocolate mints + chocolate sprinkles. The last one was Tsion and she got the wonder woman one. Tsion gave it to me 'cause I love ice cream! The wonder woman one tasted like bubble gum too. I ate my ice cream on the park bench. When we finished we went home and got ready for Sky Zone. When we were there mom jumped so high she hollered + screamed.

Malaki L.

Age 13, Concord

My Mom

My mom, loving and
caring by cooking great
meals, driving me everywhere
and talks to me.
My mom, coming in from
a hard day of work
all dressed.
My mom, a busy woman
but still has time for her
5 children.
My mom, playing games
and watching movies that
we like.
My mom, telling us to
follow our dreams; "Reach
the stars" is what she says.
My mom, telling me stories
about when she would
beat up some kids.
My mom, making the
room feel bright and alive.
My mom, when she leaves
it makes me sad but I
know I will see her bright
beautiful face again.

Trilobite

This trilobite looks like
a frog poking its head
out of the water.

The marks on it makes
it like when something
comes out of the water,
bugs swimming away.

The color of it looks
like a black top getting
put on some old gray
cement.

The Beach

When I was at the
beach it felt like
paradise.
We had so much fun
swimming in the
salty blue ocean.
Tasting the delicious
food,
Getting to be able to
go on a big Ferris
wheel,
and walking on the
long balcony over
the ocean.
Life was really good
at the beach.

Dominique D.

Age 10, Saint Florian

When I Got Hurt

The first time I busted my head open, it didn't bust open all the way. It was kind of like 4 inches but let me tell you what happened. I was coming home from the school bus stop in front of my house. My dad was waiting for me. He said, "You got to do your homework, then we will go to the store." I said ok. So I went to go do my homework. I was getting my homework done. My brother was at the table eating. So my pencil dropped. I bent over to get it. The chair fell. I hit my head. I ran upstairs crying. My dad came out of the room. He said, "What happened?"

I took my hand off my head. He looked at my hands. He rushed to the bathroom cleaning me up to stop the blood from coming. He called mommy. She left work as soon as she could. I was dizzy so when I got there. They put this thing on my finger.

Then they took me to one of the rooms. I waited and then came the doctor. He said he was going to see if I lost a lot of blood or do a test. So they told me to lay on the hospital bed. They put this stuff in my head—the staple. After they got done I cried my mom Said, "It's ok." Then we left. The doctor said we had to come back Monday, but we came back Tuesday. When we got there, They took me into one of the rooms. When they came, they took the staples out. It hurt, but I am ok. I still hurt to this day.

When Someone Tricked Me

I remember when I got played a trick on. When I went to a cousin's house to spend a night, Her brother, which is my cousin, was sleeping. I woke up. I was wet. I thought I peed on myself. SO I went to take a shower. Then my cousin said, "Dominique, You didn't pee on yourself." I said, "The heck?" Then she said, "I poured water on you."

The First Time I Ate Ribs

So it was the 4th of July. My uncle was barbecuing. So when we got there, he was cooking on the grill. He made some ribs, chicken, Hot dogs, Burgers, some egg salad and a lot more. All them flavors mixed together smelled good. So we were playing football, baseball, Volleyball and basketball. It was so fun. After that, it was time to eat. So after that we left to go to Anderson. It was not that long so when we got there, we started to play with our cousins. So my grandpop was cookin' so we went to go to see some fireworks. When we got back, we ate. It was getting dark. That's when I ate my first ribs. It was good, juicy and the bbq was so good that I want some today.

P.S. I was 5 years old.

Dylan B.

Age 9, Saint Florian

New Baby Sister

This is the story of a life changing decision. One day in April (I think) my mom said she was pregnant. I wasn't sure to be happy or sad but I could not hold it in so I was . . .

SO HAPPY!

Like a month ago we found out the baby was a girl so I'm Happy and can't wait. When she comes? Oh If you want to know when she comes it's OCTOBER!!!!

And I'm gunna be a big sister and the life changing decision is if I would be a rule sister or a do whatever sister but I found out that I should be a free and rule. What I mean by *Rule* is she can't do everything and *Whatever* means she can do whatever and I don't care.

French Fries

Funny things happen when I eat my fries. Like me being crazy because they're so good. My favorite place to get fries is Shoefly. Why? Because they have olive oil and little leaves of spinach. Why I like fries is because they make me feel fun and that's why I like them and it's all on my auntie because she gave them to me and I love her for that.

The Fourth of July

On the 4th of July in my neighborhood we have a big big block party. We had a parade and the police officer closes the road so all the kids could ride their bikes/scooters. We also had cupcakes, mint water, cookies, and lemonade. And guess what? At the parade there were horses.

Boogie Boarding

I'm writing about when I did something new/the best day ever. The best day ever is when I went to Myrtle Beach we got a beach house right by the beach. Who all went with me is my mom and dad and uncle, Aunt and cousin. Our beach house was so close it only took two minutes to get there when I ran straight to the water and guess what I did? Went boogie boarding it was so fun. Why? Because I messed up but it was still funny because it's the beach. The first time I did boogie boarding I tried to stand on it and I flipped in the water then I tried it again and went under water and floated back to shore.

Tylen C.

Age 9, Saint Florian

Best Day Ever!

My most exciting memory is when I went to Kings Island. We were in Great Wolf Lodge and Great Wolf Lodge owns Kings Island. So we got out swimming suits and went to a big waterslide. Then we went to the wave pool. Every time we tried to swim up to the deep end the wave pushed us back, so me and my cousin went back to the waves and every time we went back it pushed us back. So we got out and the wave snuck up on us and it pushed us forward and I got scraped on my hip and the water was wet and my mom came out picked me up and took me out the pool. Everybody said, "Are you okay?" I said, "No it really hurts." So my mom took a band-aid out and put it on my scrape and it felt much better then we went back to Great Wolf Lodge and put on dry clothing The went outside to get some fresh air. It smelled like chlorine. Then we got something to eat.

The best day ever!!!!!

The Playground

It all started when we were outside and I was running then this person came up on me and pushed me down. Then my friend Joey helped me up. I said thanks. Then I went to tell the teacher and she called the kid over and made him say sorry to me. He got in trouble because he refused to say sorry and could not play outside for a whole week. So I told my mom and my dad everything that happened. Then tomorrow he said sorry to me outside on the playground. I was playing tag and the kid push me over so I called out to get my friend.

Will M.

Age 12, Saint Florian

Favorite Food

My favorite food is chicken. To be specific, fried chicken. I like the smell of chicken. It smells like heaven put into the form of food. The sound of chicken of the crunchy chicken skin. The chicken tastes like...chicken. It feels like a ridged mountain range. When I put a piece in my mouth it gets all warm. When I look at chicken my mouth waters. My dad gets a Discount on the chicken on Tuesday. I usually eat chicken at home with my family.

Kid Flash and the Big Hill

My mom my brother and I went bike riding together. My brother wasn't good at riding so we had some problems. We were going to my aunt's house. Christopher would fall off the bike into someone's lawn about 5 times. Then came trouble, the big hill, Christopher's worst nightmare. The hill was steep. While me and my mom were coasting my brother was doing the weirdest thing. He was pedaling with the hill. He was going so fast it was like he was kid flash on a bike. He swerved around me fast. That's when he got hurt. Christopher fell off his bike and scraped his stomach. At first I cried because I was worried but he was fine. Then we made it to my aunt's house and we cleaned Christopher up and everything was fine.

Tamara V.

Age 13, Saint Florian

Dad's Car Accident

On May 25th at 3:00am in the morning I got a call that my Dad is in the hospital. I got up, got dressed, and me and my grandparents were heading to the hospital. When we arrived at the hospital we asked for Jerry V. Jr. They gave us his information and we went in the ER and I saw him. His eyes were closed. He couldn't talk. He had wires and tubes on him, but he was stable. The doctor said he had a lot of damage. He had brain damage, lung damage, pelvis broke, liver and bladder eruption, etc. Then a couple weeks after the doctor said he wasn't gonna make it and was gonna die. I started to cry because I had just talked to him before he went to work. He said, "I love you twin." But a few weeks later, on June 6th last day of school I went to the hospital. When I got there he was awake. I said, "Hey Dad." He said, "Hey princess." I said, "Dad!!!!!!!!! You can talk." Then the doctor came in and I had to go. Then yesterday all of his kids went to the hospital. When we got there he saw us and tried to get out the bed. Then we had to go and he gave us a huge smile and said, "I love you."

I Peed on Myself

This was the story about me peeing my pants. We were on the bus heading to a restaurant for dinner in Washington, D.C. We pulled up to Cracker Barrel. Then we had to get off the bus and line up as how old we are. After that we walked in and sat down at the tables. The room had four booths, 3 long tables, and two square tables. I sat a booth with my friends named Elexis, Marauld, Ashanti, and Breanna. My friends were telling their funny moments. My friend Elexis's story was so funny that I peed on myself. I was able to leave the restaurant right away. I went straight to the Hotel, got in the shower first, and throw my hotel party. I don't remember what the funny story was. This created a new memory for me.

The End

Regret

The time I pulled a trick on somebody. It was at Tindley Collegiate Academy in the classroom. It was August, 20, 2013. Me and my classmates were there. My friend Jordan went to throw her tissue away. While she wasn't looking I pulled the chair back. When she came back to sit down the chair was back and she fell. Everybody started laughing. I did it because I wanted to make everybody laugh. Now that I did it I regret it happened.

Elijah H.

Age 10, Saint Florian

Pizza as Big as My Hands

My fav food is Pizza. My fav topping is cheese, so much cheese that they can make a statue out of it. All the cheese in the world. My shirt reminds me of cheese. Thinking about it makes me drool. I had pizza at this camp. They bought it from Papa John's. My favorite pizza is from Subway. Eat fresh! They're as big as my hands.

The Switch Up

The last decision I had to make that was hard was rather to have a Popsicle or popcorn. I wanted to stop all the corn I been eating the last 3 days. I wanted popcorn to continue the popping. I wanted a Popsicle to stop the corn rush. My decision was neither. I got a cinnamelt and chocolate chip cookies. And after eating both of them I had a sugar rush and it took me to 3426 Southgale. My grandma said I was doing the wobble. She said, "One second I was doing the dishes, another second you was Gone!"

While I was running, my money fell out of my pocket. I was on my way home, but people was starting to take it. I stopped them from taking my money. I followed my money back home. When I got home I saw my mom almost on the phone with The Police wondering where I ran to.

Lego Spaceship

When I built the spaceship I felt awesome. It was bigger than my hand. It was 196 pieces. I was surprised. I made it in one Hour.

It was a big spaceship. I threw it up into the ceiling fan. Then it sat on the fan blade for a long time. I was playing with a Lego car, and then the spaceship fell off of the fan, and the car hit the spaceship. *BAM* the car hit the Lego. I was really surprised because there was zero chance for something like that to happen! It's important I told my story because I love Legos, because Legos started on my birthday.

Whoopsie Dayzee

I Lost my sense of freedom in summer. It started when I was 6… the first day of camp. No family, only one friend Morgan W., the problem was she was a girl so I couldn't be next to her but Later on in the camp funny things happened. A boy named Roman pranked David. Right after we all took showers we were walking back to our cabin. Roman tapped David when he had no clothes. Then he ran from him and the counselor turned on the lights. And we a saw him naked I said, "Whoopsie dayzee." David was trying to get out of the situation by taking my sleeping bag. I said, "Get your own."

Tianna C.

Age 11, Saint Florian

When I Lost Someone

One late night I was over my godmother's house and my godfather had left to go to the hospital to check on my grandmother because they had called for questions. Left at home, it was me, my mom, my godmother, and my brother. My brother was back in his room and we were in the front. I was on my phone playing games but my mom and my godmother where in the front dining room playing cards. A couple hours later, my godfather came back in tears and I had already knew what he was going to say. Everyone started growing tears and we all joined in a circle of crying and tears. That day is a day I'll never forget. One thing I'll never forget about her is that she will never let anyone punish me. She was always kind, never mean, calm, always calm. I remember those days when she would pick me up from school and we would cook meals for our dinner.

The Hilarious Day

One day in class at school, my teacher, Mr. T., was mad and yelling at us because we weren't in line and we were talking. Then his pencil dropped and when he reached down to get it his chair flew out and he fell hard on his bottom. The room went completely silent. I tried not to laugh but I couldn't hold it in. But my teacher said it was okay to laugh. Then the room filled with laughter. I had tears coming out of my eyes and I could barely breathe. Mr. T.'s face was funny and he acted like it wasn't.

I Remember...

I remember when I played a trick on somebody. It was a day after school and my mom dropped me off at home so she could go to the store. So, when she pulled up in the driveway, I ran to my hallway closet and shut the door. I tried to be quiet as I possibly could. Then I heard the door open and laughed inside but tried to be quiet as I possibly could. Then I heard the door open and laughed inside but tried to be quiet. Then my mom yelled my name to help her with the groceries. She walked down the hallway, and I banged on the door and yelled gibberish. She yelled and almost punched me. I got scared but I started cracking up laughing. She got mad at me but she was laughing on the inside. I was eleven years old when this happened.

Smashing the Pizza

I remember when I ate my favorite food. It was only yesterday when my mom picked me up from camp and I looked and I saw pizza. I wanted my mom to hurry and get home so I could eat. She tried to hurry and get home but when we pulled up in the driveway, I raced out the car and grabbed the pizza and got ready to smash the pizza. I got my plate and ate my pizza with breadsticks. The pizza was pepperoni and cheese. After that I went outside and played basketball. My mom got it from Little Caesars.

Roderick W. II

Age 9, Saint Florian

First Day at Camp

I remember the time I first came to St. Florian summer camp. I felt nervous when I walked through the door, and in the middle of the day I felt better. I felt better because I made new friends in camp. We went on a field trip and that also made me feel better. We went to the swimming pool and we had fun. We got dumped by a giant bucket above our heads. It hurt like a lot of thunderstorms going at once on your head. My friend and I went down a slide. We had to lay down and put our hands across our chests. It was dark and then I saw light. I forgot to cover my nose and I hit the water. I couldn't breathe for a second. Water went up my nose. The counselor told me to go back to the pool. So I went. And then after, I went down the small red slide and got sprayed with water. And then I went down the little yellow slide for babies. I went fast for a second. I was so low I almost got stuck and couldn't get up. The bus came and picked us up. After that we went back to summer camp. We talked about what to do Monday. Then we played on the playground and our parents picked us up from there. I was playing basketball. Then my dad picked him and he wanted me to keep playing while he talked to counselor Tim, but I was ready to go home. It was the greatest, best first day of camp I have ever had before!!!

My Favorite Food

My mom called me for dinner. She said we were having steak. I took my steak downstairs in the basement to watch TV. And my mom came downstairs and said I have to eat my green beans, too. I only ate my broccoli. My mom told me to eat my steak, too. So, I added steak sauce and I took a bite. The inside was so juicy and pink. I put so much steak sauce on it, my mouth was filled with steak. All that was left was the bone. I got seconds on steak and broccoli. It was both smoky and meaty. I was able to chew it with ease, but it was still kind of hard, too. My mom put salt and pepper. And she told me about the recipe and you have to keep the inside pink. She told me to keep it juicy inside and tender to make it taste good. And then she'll give me the rest when I grow up. She has a whole book of them from her grandma. It has the steak in there. One day the book will be mine. I ate a lot of steak. I almost eat it every time I go to my mom's house. She makes it special for me and for cookouts with the family. She might make it for the 4th of July. But I hope she doesn't because I don't like bugs on my steak. Bugs are nasty on my steak. It doesn't taste right on my steak. You never know where the bugs go. They might pee on people's faces or ears. I like soda with my steak. I don't know why? I like Dp. Dp stand for Dr. Pepper or sprite. Those are my favorite sodas. Soda tastes like pop rocks in your mouth, but more taste.

Adidas Scar

I was at school and it was recess time. I was playing tag. I went down the slide and there were two girls my friend pushed them down the slide and my hands were sideways and my skin got cot in the slide and I got a scratch. And my friend got one too, but his is on his elbow and it doesn't look like Adidas sign. Mine looks like an Adidas sign.

Nia D.

Age 9, Saint Florian

Chicken

My favorite food is chicken because when I was moving into my new house me and some of my family had chicken. It was from Jordan's fish and chicken. It was good. After that we finished putting everything away. Then everybody left and we ate the rest of the chicken. The rest was for the next day.

Caribbean Cove

Yesterday I went to Caribbean Cove. I got a giant bucket of water dumped on my head. Then I got sprayed by a fake turtle that you can slide on. I went down a waterslide and I went to a hot tub and the lazy river. My cousins were with us but my cousin's sister had to work. When we were in the big pool my brother had to stay on the steps because the water was too deep. I had fun that day and I want to go back again.

Girl Scouts

The best day of my life was when I got promoted to a Junior in Girls Scouts. When my Girl Scout troop took a picture my friend was doing weird poses and my other friend was just staring at her. Then the adults and our brothers sprayed us with water guns.

Raccoon in the Attic

I remember when there was a raccoon in the Attic. It was a baby. I named it Zaeda. We found it when the Guy came and he set a trap and the next day the raccoon was in the trap. Then the man came to get the raccoon but he said that she might come back.

Trevon I.

Age 12, Concord

Me

I am a tall boy 5'7" and love to play basketball, but
on my free time I like to spend time with my
family. I love to go to school because I like
the way we share ideas and interact with
each other. At school I'm having fun, but at
home I talk to my parents, showing a lot
of expression, and even though we have downfalls,
we always push through it.

My Room

The dark as I walk in my room I feel comfortable. The
dark thunderstorms pass through. The dark
dark, a lonely place where I can think.
A dark place where there's always silence, a
place where your mind flows.

Gourd

Hard texture
round like the
moon, as rough
and gold as
corn flakes. As
sensitive as glass,
Thinking I'm responsible.

Reggie T.

Age 12, Saint Florian

Middle School

The first day of middle school was August 6, 2013, and I woke up nervous. I got out of bed and walked to the bathroom. I took a shower then brushed my teeth. After that I walked back to my room and put on a light blue shirt, camo shorts, light blue Derrick Rose socks, and my Derrick Rose 773s. I went downstairs, ate 2 s'mores pop tarts then watched TV until the bus came at 7:45. At 7:39 I turned off the TV then walked outside to the bus stop and waited till 7:45. At 7:48 the bus stopped in front of me. I got on, then walked towards the back of the bus where my friends from 5th grade Bobby and Todd sat. We drove to school and the bus driver asked for all 7th graders to get off first. The 7th graders got off the bus then walked into the school, then he asked all 6th graders to get off the bus. As I got off the bus I got excited because I saw a lot of my friends from Elementary school.

The Decision

The time I made a hard choice was when I had to choose between getting the game *Littlebigplanet 2* or *WWE 2K14*. My friend Edriece wanted me to get *Littlebigplanet 2* because we both like adventure games and you can play with people around the world. Plus Edriece and I can both play together and create our own worlds. We can also play scary pop out levels where the creators of the game make scary worlds to try to scare the players. My other friend, Jalen, wanted me to get *WWE 2K14*. It's a wrestling game that he likes to play and he recommended it to me. He said, "You have *WWE 1, WWE Network* and you watch *WWE* every Monday and Friday."

Kobe

My favorite pair of shoes are called the Kobe Venomenon 4s. I got them in April and my mom took me to Foot Locker to get them. When we walked into Foot Locker I immediately knew the ones I wanted. I got the Kobes off of the shelf but there were 15 people in line in front of us. So we went to Champs to get the shoes. I walked into Champs, and as soon as my foot touched the floor, employees were asking me, "Can I help you?" So I said, "Yes I am looking for the Kobe Venomenon 4s." They went to the back.

Tyree D., Jr.

Age 8, Saint Florian

Jump from 2 Story Window

I remember the time I jumped out of a 2 story window and did not a break leg. This girl was about to steal my bike so I jumped out of a 2 story window. It was my cousin's house. It was a huge house but not big enough to be a mansion. I was standing by the window, and the girl got mad at me because she lost a game to me. The girl is driving my bike off trying to take it to her house around the corner. I was angry and I wanted my bike back. I didn't even think when I jumped out of the window. I didn't even know I did it. I was scared. It hurt when I hit the ground. It felt like I was still going when I hit the ground. My cousin drove me on the 4 wheeler to get my bike back and I felt happy.

Danger Dude

I got the scar on my hand from Kings Island. My dad calls me "danger dude." The scar came from a log that goes up and down that had twist and turns. My whole family went. When my hand hit the ride. I started crying. It felt like a door fell on my hand. When I got hurt it got better the next day. The sore does not hurt and it is see-through.

New Pair of Jordans

One week there were these new pair of Jordans. But they were 200 Bucks. I went to the mall with 80 dollars and bought 67 dollars shoes. They were Black and Red. I played basketball in them with my friend and my dad. The shoes felt very comfortable. I played very well that day. Then went over my daddy's. He took me to his mom's, took care of her 'cause she was sick. Made 100. Went home, help this dude move in, another 100+100=200. Bought the new Jordans had no more money after that, which made me sad. On the bright side, I had new Jordans.

Victor G.

Age 12, Concord

"La Siesta" *By Vincent Van Gogh*

White old people lay on
a big pile of hay stack
with shoes and scythes
beside them while
they sleep because of
how tired they are.
They are tired because
of all the hay they have cut.

Geode

Any time I see a geode it
reminds me of somebody
smashing a lot of diamonds
and putting them in a
rock. The back is
like you're taking a
hike and feeling little
rocks on your shoe
but now they are on your fingers.

Remember Me

I want to be remembered
by a statue made of gold
with me celebrating
a goal that I had just made.
My hands high in the air
and my house right next to it
so people can see where I
lived when I was a kid.

Savannah N.

Age 7, Saint Florian

What I Like About my Neighborhood

I get to play with my best friends F1 and F2. We play tag and hide
and seek, go outside—find the friend and smack in the face.
My house has stairs and is white.
I live where the middle is.
My pet fish died because my mommy
didn't let me feed her.
I live with Serenity, Joshua, and Charnile.

Day at the Fair

My day at the fair, I went on the rollercoaster. There was poop everywhere from the horses and pigs. They jumped out of their cages. People were talking and the horses were marching. It was like 90 something degrees. I got on a swing on a playground and jumped off the swing and got back on. The roller coaster was a zig zag jumping over and people were screaming, including me. That was so crazy. Next we got on the racing cars. I picked a pink car that had hearts, diamonds, stars, and sparkles. I heard my mom, dad, and brother cheering for me. On the other hand, my big sister was chanting, "I hate Savannah." I think she was just jealous that she didn't race. It was only $2.00. I then heard, "On Your Mark, Get Set, Go!" I took off and I was in the lead.

My Cut

I remember… When I first cut my fingers! I was at my mommy's house! I put a piece of tissue on my fingers. I was trying to peel an orange and I cut my fingers with a sharp knife. My mommy put alcohol on it and she wrapped it up! I cried so hard it hurted!

Frozen Yogurt

This is the story of when I went to Miche's. We got frozen yogurt, and ice cream mixed together. It was cake batter and chocolate chip with sour patch, gummy worms, more chocolate chips and a sucker on top. I shared it with my younger brother.

Ice Cream!

There's ice cream all over the place at The Chocolate Cafe. Auntie, uncle, and mommy took me, Serenity, Josh, and Charlie. I got some birthday cake batter ice cream. It was pink, purple, green, orange, red, and gold! The ice cream was 1 degrees! It was so cold outside, like 35° and we got some ice cream. So then we went to the hotel and took some pictures. And then I ate some more ice cream. I just stuffed my face. It was chocolate and strawberry and vanilla mixed. The end.

Jocelyn R.

Age 13, La Plaza

The Time Music was in My Life

The time music was in my life. Well I was in 7th grade and I was in choir. Well I didn't know what it was. I was so nervous that I was shaking like I was in a very cold place with shorts and a shirt. I didn't know where the class was, so I was asking everyone like crazy. Once someone showed me where the class was. I felt so shy because I didn't know what we were going to do in the class. I open the cold door. Everyone was staring at me, I had all the attention. The class room was so cold. I had the chills.

So I went to my chair. The chair was cold and hard. So the teacher was taking about what the class is about. She introduced herself to the class. Her name was Mrs. Good. After that she teached us the music notes and what the music notes were called. At first I was so confused. A weekend passed and there was a test about the music notes. I was so nervous that I was gonna fail. I felt bubbles in my stomach. The teacher was passing out the test and every time the test was getting closer to me. I felt the pressure get bigger and bigger. Then was finally in front of my face. I was looking at the test and I started to do the test. I think it was kinda hard. I thought I didn't know none of the notes. There was music notes that the teacher did not teach us. So I was like the 5th person to be done. I was so nervous.

It was Monday and I went to choir. I was so sleepy that I was gonna pass out. I had that morning taste when you wake up in the morning. So the test was on my desk. The teacher said, "Good job." I was thinking that I didn't fail now I slowly graved the test. I looked at my test. I got a 100% A+. I was so happy. I started to dance. I was the only one that got an A+ on that test. I felt so proud of myself. I just notice that I had the music in me. I'm glad that I was in that class. I may not be a good singer but I love to dance. I would Dance to the beat. I would have to know all the notes to sing. I think I'm not a good singer but others may think.

Heroes

A hero is someone who saves people.
A hero is someone who is honest.
A hero is someone who helps.
A hero is a leader.
People has their own hero in their lives.

Mom and Dad is a hero
My friends is a hero
teachers are heroes
family is a hero
food is my hero

I am a hero

Letter to a Hero

Dear mom,

You're my hero because you've been there my whole life. You took care of me since I was small. You gave me something that meant a lot to me now. It's changed my life. You taught me about things in school and at home.

Randy B.

Age 13, La Plaza

Admiration

My mom has done so much I would fill this entire page and more. My mom's name is Paola. She might not have the best name but I believe she is a better mom than yours. If I would have told you how many things my mom have told me it would be too darn nice. My mom always supports me in everything I do, unless it's stupid. My family sometimes come to my soccer games. Do you know who invites them? You guessed wrong my mom invites my family. I love the way that my mom cheers more than my family combined. My mom is my fan, not really. My mom constantly takes me to soccer practice at Avon. Soccer practice is on Monday, Wednesday and Friday. She is my role model. Every time I went to practice before that I went to the gas station and bought a slushie.

My Journey towards My Soccer Career

I played for U.S.A.I. United Soccer Alliance of Indiana. My coach was happy that I joined. He scouted me when I was in recovery. Now I'm traveling to places I never thought I'd been like Tennessee, Kansas, Illinois, Michigan, Maine and South Carolina.

Cristiano Ronaldo is my mentor because Ronaldo is my Idol. He might not be the best player but the way he plays is beast. Ronaldo is the most criticized player in the world.

I Am the Wolf

I am the wolf!
My name means brave.
I am fast, brave, and strong.
I wonder if I should eat the deer or not?
I hear a howl.
I see a wolf.
I taste meat.
I smell nature.
I feel the blood in my mouth.
I want some food.
I was a helpless turtle.
I am a wolf
I will be a useless metamorphic human.
I pretend to be a wolf.
I feel scared when I get close to a bear.
I feel weak when I'm not with my pack.

Pumpkin Cake

As soon as I got this beautiful piece of cake. Wait, wait, wait, not just a piece of cake; it's a masterpiece. It looks like a cake model with vanilla sprinkles. The cake itself looks like a soft sponge. It smells like sugar and candy mixed. The first time I tried the moist piece I ate a bit and rapidly kept eating it as I finished I said please come back and almost cried :'(I dream about pumpkin cake sometimes but when I do I have it by my side all the time.

Collaborative Poem

Concord

"Central Library"
Indianapolis

Outside, there was a big black doughnut
on the wall—a sculpture called
"Thin Man Little Bird." We saw
Egyptian animals and Greek gods
in the stone.

Inside, it was old, big and unexpected.
The gold bars we slid on
looked like shiny metal
and smelled like new silver.

The new section was an artistic
creation. Neon lights
changed from green to blue
to light blue, and the poles
were like monkey bars.

Lauren C.

Age 7, Saint Florian

When the Two Sisters Fighted

I remember when my sister told her friend that I dig in my boogers I felt sad when she told her friend I was crying. While I was crying I was embarrassed that was the embarrassing moment of my life. And then she tells secrets to her friend. I felt really really sad. And I get really really mad. Even though I get mad, I still love my sister because we're family. And family never ever ever doesn't like family.

Cinderella Bear

One day Kailey, My sister and me were fighting about Build-A-Bear.

"Give it Back," and she said, "No."

She sat on the Top bunk bed and she took off the Cinderella dress and put it on her bear and then the dress fell behind the bed. Then I climbed down the bunk bed and then I went in the living room and left. The Build-A-Bear with my sister. But I didn't give her permission to undress my bear. But I wasn't angry anymore because we shouldn't fighted in the first place. She didn't have to do that and I didn't care in the first place and we're not even suppose to fight, I mean we didn't even have to. After that she gave my bear back to me.

Pizza

I love pizza. And I like my pizza with pepperoni and cheese and I get my pizza from Pizza Hut. It is shaped like a triangle.

My favorite shoes are twinkle toes. They light up pink. They are green and have stripes. They're like stripes with glitter on them. Lots and lots of glitter! And that's my story.

Marquia T.

Age 12, Saint Florian

My 8 Year Old Scar

When I was four years old my relatives and I went over my uncle Jason's house, and I was playing chase with my slightly older cousin, Jaden. I guess Jaden was *it*, and since she was older she was also faster. Jaden once tagged me so now I'm the tagger.

I'm running down the sidewalk, hoping I'll be at the edge of her tennis shoes... then my flat was hugging the tiny rocks beneath my feet which made gravity take control of me. I skinned my knee up on the sidewalk in front of my auntie old house. So, now I'm just lying there on the hot sidewalk, screaming.

At that time I didn't know what to do & I could tell Jaden didn't either. I ended up in my Grandmother's big yellow house, sitting on her foot stool. Tears coming down my cheeks, Eyes puffy red, and a sting of rubbing alcohol being slapped on my open wound.

I stayed in Grandmother's house for a while, mainly because walking just wasn't going to happen. I'm twelve now but if you look at my left knee, that 8 year old scar still lives. The End

I Remember

Joining LaNique Expressions Dance Co.
When we did our first showcase
Sliding on sweat during practice
Joining Anointed Expressions of Christ (AEOC)
When he practiced a lot on one song
Thinking about giving up on one dance in LaNique
Performing at Black Expo with AEOC

You Annoying

This morning I was gelling my hair down and my little brother, Jordan, came into the restroom with me and urinated. So, I threw some water on my hairbrush and a little water got on my hand.

My brother needed to wash his hands so I sort of helped him by giving him some soap and turning on the water faucet. Once I finally put on my hair tie in and dried my hands off, Jordan started to cry for no apparent reason.

I wanted to hurt him so bad. First, because he was just standing there in my presence. Second, cause he wouldn't communicate with me when I asked what was wrong. Third, because he got louder once I left out the restroom.

Marlene R.

Age 14, La Plaza

My Favorite Food

My favorite food is beans. I like all different kinds of beans. The beans I normally eat are in a can and all I do is put it in a pan and put the pan on the stove then I wait until they boil. Then after that I would put it on a bowl and get Mozzarella cheese and put it on top and wait until it melts and then I eat it. I don't really know why I really like it.

Beans have been my favorite food since I was little. My mom said that when I was little and we lived in Mexico every time I ate beans I would have them all over my face. The first time she told me that I just laughed. But honestly I don't think I would survive without beans. I think that when I grow up and have my own house and have to get my own food. I would always have beans at my house.

I guess that I like beans because all you have to do is boil them. And I really don't like to cook plus I don't I guess it's because I'm just too lazy to cook plus I don't really think it's my thing. I like when people cook for me but I don't like cooking for people or myself. Plus every time I cook at home my brother always has to kill my vibe by telling me that I always burn the food and it always ends up tasting bad. But there is just one thing that I don't like about beans it's that it makes me gassy. And that is really bad because if I eat a lot of beans it makes my stomach hurt and when I get gassy it smells like rotten eggs and it's just nasty. But I don't care I still and will always like beans. And that's why my favorite food is beans.

Strong independent Future

When I think about my future, I think of me being a strong and independent person. I see myself as what I always wanted to be that is a lawyer. A person that represents other people to help them get to justice. I picture myself with a house not too big or small. With a small dark blue car. I feel that in the future I would be a more helpful person then I am now. I would not be only helpful to my friends and families but also to call the people that need that help.

I know I'm Latino because I have lots of family members. Lots of them don't get along. But since the world we live in is not that big so I see lots of my tios, tias, and primos everywhere. I have some cousins that I don't even know existed. Or some of my so-called uncles are not even related to me. For example my favorite Uncle Miguel is not really my uncle but we still treat them like family. Even if we are mad at each other we still got each other's back.

My Special Place

My special place is my room because it's mine and that's like my thinking place. I'm in my room mostly all day. I'm in there when I'm mad and I just throw everything everywhere. I go in my room when I am bored because as soon as I enter my room I see something unorganized so I start organizing it and it makes time go by fast and it takes my boredom away. Also, I always have paper and markers so sometimes I just go in there in draw! When I'm in my room I can be myself I can sing, dance, jump, play ex without my mom yelling at me. If someone is in my room I kind of boss them around because they are like in my space where only I can say what you can do and what you can't. I say what goes where in my room if I want to change something I will. I don't have to ask anyone if I can. I make up my own rules in my room.

I like my room because its big I have a couch a TV that I watch when I don't have nothing to do. I go to my desk that's like on the right of the room next to the TV and the couch. I go to my desk to draw and do my homework or sometimes I bring food inside my room so I just set down on my little wooden desk and eat. I go in room to get my clothes from my little closet on the far end of my room. I go to my room to sleep on my little bed with my purple blankets. My bed is right in front of my door so right when you open the room that's like the first thing you would see. All around my room I have pictures like pictures from when I was little and pictures of my family. But there is this one picture on the top of my desk that I look to think about what I have done in life and I have to live life to the extreme because you never know when your life will end. That picture in my room is the picture of my aunt that died in Mexico, and I look at it to remember the things we did together.

Joshua C.

Age 9, Saint Florian

Joshua the Super Hero

It was Thursday, at Capital City IPA School. We were in the classroom and my second-grade teacher Mrs. Bailey was over sharpening pencils and I asked her why were you under there? And she said underwear Then we all laughed. So time past, and as soon as we got to lunch. So when my best friend came and offered me a snack. Then it was just a paper towel in the package. Soon time past and it was graduation. My friends and I came downstairs...

I remember this story I made up called: "Joshua The Super Hero."

It was a fine day in the city of Porkbelly. Jonny came out the door and said, "Josh, come and teach me how to be a super hero." "I can't," said Joshua. Susuan and Mory came out the house and looked mad. Suddenly Bling Bling Boy came out and used his storm powers. The sky started raining and hailing and a hurricane started to form. Joshua came out and changed into his super suit. Then Joshua came out the mobile and flew into the air and used his storm power. "Alert alert!" "Joshua, it's Susuan?" "You need to find your way back in no time to spare." "PU dad this meat loaf is nasty," said Joshua. Bang 321 bam. "Jonny." Joshua went upstairs and told on Jonny. Soon Dukey came in with a piece of staek. Joshua saw his signal and jumped in his super cave. He knew he had to go to Bling Bling island, he didn't see BB Boy. BBB had went to the store and stole some Red Gush, "WHAT," Jonny said. Joshua went to the store where BBB was and had stopped him. Susuan and M Mary waited outside. BBB went inside and took EVERYTHING they had. Joshua was waiting at the bank with all his traps. BBB went and took Joshua to his Jail. Joshua soon got out but BBB got him back. Will Joshua ever escape and save the day?

To be continued

Joseph A.

Age 6, Saint Florian

Dog

I got a new toy. It was a monster truck race track. It was awesome. And a ball track. I play with them a lot. I have a dog named Bud. He goes on the table and dives in the swimming pool. I got 4 birds, but we can't let them out of the cage. But I can give them bird food. There is a door for it. It all makes me happy. All the things I have make me happy and happier than I could be. I play with my dog and teach him tricks. Spin around, jump, and catch a tennis ball. And I say, "Go fetch, Dog!" The dog wakes me up. And the dog sleeps in my room. Whenever I feel alone, Bud keeps me company. He is the best dog ever. And the birds, too. They chirp in the summer time. There is going to be baby birds. I saw eggs in the cage and they are starting to hatch. I have a pet owl. It hooted at bedtime. It is a white snowy owl. And there are baby owls. They know the schedule.

New York

It was night time and it was the 4th of July. All the people who were living in Indianapolis had to move to New York because every firefighter was too tired to fight the fires. They made an announcement: "If you want to see the fireworks you have to go to New York on the 4th of July." They even had to take Chuck E. Cheese and Toys R Us and all the stores that were fun. They had to put them all on three airplanes and they had to be dropped off at New York. It moved so fast to the airport. We were going so fast that we heard it stop. *Screeeeech*!

Joseph

J I **j**umped on the trampoline
O I ate a **ora**nge
S I was a **s**nake
E I ate **e**ggs
P my balloon **P**OP!
H it w**h**at
A the **a**nd

Luis L.

Age 18, La Plaza

I Am

I am Luis
My name mean Luigi the Glowing Flame
I am friendly, kind, smart, shy
I wonder why I don't have fun sometimes
I hear when people talk to me
I see a good report card
I taste sweet peaches
I smell air conditioners
I feel happy
I want to be a mechanic
I was an eleventh grader
I am a jokester
I will be kind to everyone always
I pretend to be someone's brother in need
I feel scared when something goes wrong in my family
I feel weak when I can't change something when I would like to
I feel strong when I know I can do something
I hope that my family will be fine
I dream that God will give me a lot of cars
I am Luis

My Family

Whenever I am sad my family is always there when I need them. My family is always nice to me and I help my mom, dad, two sisters, and brother every time they need me. My mom and dad are kind to us kids and extended family. My sister Laura is really smart and likes to do homework. Anamarie is soft-spoken until you make her mad. If she loses control she will curse and say hurtful words. My brother Javier is a jokester that does funny pranks. When mom is in a bad mood he keeps telling jokes until he makes her laugh. As a family we go to church on Saturday, watch movies, and play soccer together. The smallest of the family is our dog Baby. She is big, white, and covered with fur. Baby plays with her white and yellow tennis ball that she fetches and either keeps or ignores.

Never Say Never

I learned this from Karate Kid. When the Karate Kid was getting beat up at the tournament he never gave up. Because, um, when I was feeling the same way as him I told the teacher and it stopped. Some kid a little bit older than me would pick on me. He tried to get me in trouble by tossing stuff at the teacher and saying it was me. He would pick on me in the hallway. After I told the teacher she asked others about what I told her. They told her I was telling the truth.

Lenabel T.

Age 13, La Plaza

One Thing about Me

I have been here more than once
I love this place
I feel the most comfort here
I can be myself when I am here.
This is my favorite place to be.
Everything I need is in this place.
Sometimes it is boring.
I have to take good care of this place.

Coloring

When I first colored inside of the lines in a coloring book, I knew I was an artist. Looking at the picture after I was finished it made me feel so proud, it made me know that patience and concentration could teach me things. Once I knew I could do it the first time, I kept on doing it and practicing to get better. As I went on with the coloring book it got more and more challenging because parts to color got smaller and there were more parts to color. As I got a little older, my age group had stopped coloring in coloring books, and they started to draw things. Since everyone in my class was doing it, I decided to try it out. At first it was so horrible I almost gave up.

It looked so terrible, it was like a deformed monster, and I hated it. Trying to draw a girl, but it turned out being ratchet. I stopped to look at my friend as they were drawing so I could get ideas, to help me out. I was in school, during free time in a classroom. I was seven years old. Everyone was doing this, so I wanted to join them too. I started practicing and I got better. Soon, I became so good at it that every time we have an art project, everyone would look at me to help them.

In the future I see myself as an artist, I see myself as a successful architect. I imagine myself creating beautiful buildings and sights. I would like to do this because it's my dream job.

In school I didn't think before I said things but the stupid things I said, didn't mean anything because to me it was just a joke but to the people around took it so seriously. This girl was sitting on the classroom couch with some of her friends and I. She kept moving side to side like something was bothering her. She had stopped on one and tried to play it off. She farted right next to me and I called her out. Everyone stood up and laughed at her. I felt bad for the couch, because the fart was kind of stinky. She started to cry and told on me. I got in trouble and the teacher told me to be respectful and I had to apologize.

First Time I Rode My Bike

It was the summer of 2007 and my family was having a cookout in the front yard. My older brothers were riding their bikes and so was I. I was getting bored of the training wheel on my bike because they were crooked and I had always slanted to one side. I asked my dad to take off my training wheels and I was super excited, I thought it would be easy, but I thought wrong. It is so hard and I got mad each time I failed to ride my bike correctly. Then my oldest brother helped me out and pushed me down a hill super fast I panicked but then I realized if I stay calm I won't fall, and I rode right. Then I was happy.

What is Latino?

I knew I was latino from the start, I just didn't know how. I remember all the traditions we did, some I questioned but some I thought were really creative and fun. I remember telling all my friends I was born in Indiana and that I was Mexican but all of that was never true. As I got a little older, I realized I never asked my parents about our culture or about them. One day I asked my mom if we were "Mexican." She laughed and told me no. She told me we're Salvadorian. Then I asked her where was I born, she responded, "New York," I was so shocked. I couldn't believe what she had told me and I was so amazed and I felt cooler. After she had told me that, I felt even prouder, if that's even a word, to be latino.

Lauren H.

Age 9, Saint Florian

Camp

I remember when my friend's friend Andrew was throwing rocks and he hit me in my knee. I fell and cried. I was really in pain and was so my other friend Joey helped me back inside of the building and got some Ice And It was at my camp Jewel.

And then He took me back outside and then I went on the big tire. The tire is a tire connected to chains and then we went inside of the building I sat out because at that point It really started to hurt. Let me tell you Andrew Is this guy whose farts smell.

I Remember

Once there was a dog that chased me. It was a German Shepherd and it was in house the owner was always playing hockey and was always denting his garage he scares me and yesterday like five people and swam in the pool in the back yard for like 2 hours or so.

He is cray cray!!!

The Best Day Ever

I remember when I went to my friend Alena's house and we both had a sleepover. Alena's brother Xavier that is four wanted to sleep with us. Because he thinks I'm his "girlfriend." But I'm 5 years older than him anyway I slept in his room with Mrs. Camile (Both of their moms) Slept in the other bed with him. (P.S. The only reason I Slept over Is because we just came Back from a Fifth Harmony concert (P.P.S. we got Suite 44 autograph). It was cool and awesome at the same time. After the concert started we had to ride a 6 person bike and we all had a great time and a awesome time after that we had a picnic with Pizza and pop at the concert I had a pretzel But Mrs. Camille did not take me my friend Jaya and Jaya's mom (Mrs. Tammy – took me). Back to Xavier But Before he left he had a hizzy fit. So I finished my pretzel then we watched a *Monster High* movie and It was about 1 a.m. So I fell asleep and Alena still watched It and then I woke up at like 8:45 and we went back to sleep and then I watched the rest of the movie!!! and then we got up and played and got breakfast and then we washed up, got dressed and then we played Project Runway and then we had the best time ever and then my mom picked me up and then I left I said, "Bye Bye." Goal REACHED.

Nakaih H.

Age 11, Saint Florian

The Dog

One day I was riding my bike down the street and I saw this really big dog I was so terrified because the fence like 3in tall and the dog was like 5 feet tall. Then I thought to myself should I turn around and go the other way or should I keep going and speed up, so I decided to turn around then my dad yelled "Kaih come on he is not going to jump over the fence," so I turned around and rode past the dog as quickly as possible.

My Cousin's Truck

Something that made me really mad was when my cousin made me cut my arm on his truck. We were helping my Grandma move her stuff to my house. I was leaning on the back of the truck when these spikey things scratched me! The truck was his light Brown Dodge Ram. They were very sharp and caused me to snatch my arm up and towards my body. It started to drip blood from the middle of the scratch and no one would give me a band-aid. I told Idrio I needed one and he said something crazy. I asked my mom, dad, and three uncles and no one would listen.

Mystery Pneumonia

One day when I went on a field trip at school to the Benjamin Harrison house. We learned that Benjamin Harrison died from pneumonia, then I went back to school with a fever of 100.8. Then I went home I felt so bad I felt lightheaded and I was really hot so my mom took me to Walgreen to get medicine the medicine was so gross it taste really thick and sweet like syrup, the bottle was like a 3D triangle the labels were blue with lots of words on them like how much to take and how many ounces there are. I hated it because I had to take it every four hours. The next day I went to the doctor's office and the doctor said that I need to just take an Advil and see if that will lower the fever. But it did not do it my temperature shot up like a rocket going to space my fever was at 104.8 my mom took me to the emergency room at St. Vincent children's hospital at 12:00. I went to a register room with this tall lady with all white on, she put a heart rate monitor on my figure the red light on the monitor it was like it was scanning my finger then she put the blood pressure thing on my arm it squeezed my arm so tight I thought it was going to stop my blood circulation. Then I waited in the waiting room, then the nurse put the door open and called my name very loud "NAKAIH" I went to a room the doctor came and talked to me and made me pee in a cup when he took the cup he said I will be back at soon as possible. Then the doctor finally came back and said you have pneumonia. He gave my mom a prescription and said you need to take this for 10 days. That's why I have medicine so I wouldn't die like Benjamin Harrison.

Hope L.

Age 9, Saint Florian

The Day I Lost My Uncle

It was a Saturday when I was at church and my sisters were at dinner somewhere and then I had to leave home. And then when I got home, I saw the ambulance and the fire truck. My sister said I think we should go home now. When they came I was crying to death. Then we had to go to my grandpa's house. Then, we came home my mother was on the phone and told us the bad news that he died. I laid on my sister's lap as she wiped my tears. Then on Sunday, I went to his funeral. The people said good and sad things about him. Then it was my turn. I could not say a word, because I started to cry. Then it was over so then we ate. Then I went to my cousin's house. She cheered me up. Then we went to sleep and as I was sleeping I thought about the good things about him. His name was Ray. I loved it when he cooked and had slippers when I woke up and then it was morning. Then we left. Me and my uncle watched movies together and we cooked together.

The Day I Got Mad

One day someone made me really mad and do you want me to tell you who that someone was? My brother. He grabbed my doll and ripped the leg off and I got so mad at him I screamed and broke one of his toys and that toy was his motorcycle Toy. He started to cry and do you want to know how I broke his toy? I grabbed the head off. Then my mother heard him so I got in trouble and got yelled at. Then I had to go to my room so then when my brother came upstairs to the room, I said in a quiet voice, "I will get you" and he ran.

Honey

I remember when my dog was a puppy. Her name was Honey. But I don't know where she came from but I got her on my birthday. Hold on PAUSE I remember where she came from: Chicago, so okay press PLAY. Ok so where were we? Right, so Honey lives in Chicago. Honey helps me when I was sad by licking my face. And she plays with me and she lays on me. We both like to sing "Father Abraham." She's not that good. She is brown. Her ears are brown. She's white like a snowball climbing off a tree. And her paws are small and white. She barks people that's at the door. She always growls at mom when she puts her in the cage. She likes biting my hair. I don't know why. Whenever I'm on the ground reading Junie B Jones, she bites my hair. And when I stand up she's still hanging on.

Joniece L.

Age 10, Saint Florian

Dog Chasing

My mom was coming home from the store. I was with her. That dog came toward us from across the street
Trying to get in the car but It did not, and Trying to get in
My Gate
But it did not my mom and I were Chased By a Black and White Pitbull. I told the dog to get on somewhere and then It Left. Next time I'm calling the animal control.
The dog was a grown up.

Food

My favorite food is everything I like fried foods, Baked foods, grilled food, Breakfast foods. Lunch foods, Chinese foods, dessert foods. I do not like coffee cake at all because it has too much caffeine in it. But it is still good but I am a food eater a lot but it is good. I like chicken, fish, and that's it. At Steak N' Shake it is not fun to wait for the foods but the food is good. Chicken fingers from Steak N' Shake is good! Milk Shakes! have flavor Chocolate It's my favorite.

Tonsils

I got my Tonsils out, and ear Tubes put in my ears. I was two years old I had to get up at 5:00 so I will be early I was getting ready to go to St. Vincent, Peyton Manning children's hospital. They gave my mom a hospital gown so I can put it on. I scared me at first but when it was 8:00 am they said time for your brain screen before the brain screen they put needles in my arm It hurt! Then they asked me what flavor I want to go to sleep. I said apple then they put the mask over my face & I was out of it. I could not hear, see, or feel nothing at all. Than I was done in about 20 minutes. I started crying from waking up. They had an ice pack over my neck before I left the hospital they said always eat ice cream. When I got home I was in pain I was hungry. I went back to sleep. The End.

Kailey P.

Age 6, Saint Florian

Vampirate Boots

I remember when I was wearing my favorite shoes while I was wearing my Vampirates (It's half vampire, half pirate) costume while I was listening, and dancing, and singing to Kidz Bop 25. I was wearing my brown high heels 'cause they're kind of like boots.

Twisted Leg

I remember when I twisted my leg yesterday. I was trying to do what my sister was doing, my sister was trying to make a hug on her mom who is my step-mom. I tried to do it too while she was doing it. I was swirling around her leg and my sister was too and I twisted my leg. It was twisted like my leg was up but not standing up. I felt like my leg bone was broke.

Trick

I remember when my dad played a trick on me because it was my bedtime and after I said prayer my dad tried to kiss me and then my dad said, "There's a bug in the room." It wasn't real because my dad was just trying to kiss me and my head was under the blanket. And then he made me get out of my blanket and he kissed me! But I did not like it because it's gross.

Charnell Peters

Student Teacher, Concord and Saint Florian

Honestly

With honesty comes a vulnerability that I don't usually like to inhabit. I've always struggled to be honest with myself, to others, and to God, and usually the best way for me to be open is through the process of writing. When I was working with the students at St. Florian and Concord, I was surrounded by bold honesty for a few hours, whether they were honestly intrigued or honestly uninterested in the work they had before them.

Concord, especially, was full of students who weren't afraid to say and write what they meant. We worked with poetry and encouraged them to find a new path for their words— one that drew on connections and comparisons, bringing together seemingly disparate ideas, words, sounds, and feelings.

Sometimes, a stick would only be described as a stick. It was brown like a stick. It was hard like a stick. But sometimes the sky was like a tsunami, and the sounds of nature made a love song, and a mother was a beautiful and strong provider. Sometimes, their wielding of language was stunning.

We got to share our own poetry with the students on many occasions, and during one session, I read to them this poem I had written:

"A Picture of Childhood Dreams"

Checkered dress and long braids blow
In changing winds of playground scene
In city park away from road.
There, the children grow their dreams on blackest eyelashes,
Bat them at every passing stranger
And onto concrete courts—
A breathing graffiti,
A living mural of swirled jazzy tones
Of orange and brown and tan people
With soul songs in them,
With purple robes and proud swinging, strutting,

Violin bows and music notes buzzing overhead,
And people just dancing and grinning and being smart
With ladies in red lipstick and slicked down parts in wavy hair
like the side of the brick building on Jay Street.
A chalk walk with jumps, skips, and cracks,
Fastest double dutching feet, and them mean boys
From Grandma's street with their growling dog,
These own everything but the eyelashes,
Because dreams are like dust but fairy-breathed,
And everyone knows fairies don't breathe on eyelashes.
They're too busy making nations of friendships
Formed on sidewalk borders,
Giving strength to walk tall and high and say what you mean
To make all them grown ups
See this is me now.
And this is who I'll be someday:
One of those people on the mural
With the long brown braids and the trumpet
floating over my head.
When I grow up I'm gonna be
What the fairies made and the red-lipped ladies said,
Everyone I want to be and nobody I don't.

After the class, a student came up to me and said I was a very good writer. I thanked her and congratulated her on her own poem that I loved. She wouldn't read it out loud, herself, but it deserved to be shared. We had a conversation about writing. She described the stories she had written and how she loves to use her imagination, and I think her eyes would have been shining with excitement had I been able to see them, but her head was down for most of the talk.

I realize that I was just like her 8 years ago, filled with a love for language that I didn't know how to share with others. And the poem I wrote is a description of me as a child, dreaming away days, thinking of who I would be, and hoping that I would turn out the way I wanted—as a writer.

"This is me now. And this is who I'll be someday." I wrote this because we live in that statement at every stage of our lives. When I was younger, I never thought that I'd be bold enough to share a poem or teach students the value of their words. I never thought that I'd be in this place, encouraging someone who reminded me of myself and wanting so badly for her to be proud of her art.

Toward the end of our time together, I watched as this student took a big breath, tucked her hair behind her ear, apologized for her nerves, and shared her poem in Author's Chair. It was amazing to watch her share her words, to accomplish what she had not previously believed to be possible.

Many times, I would hear, "this is stupid" or "I'm not good at this," because they honestly thought they were bad, and it was a privilege to tell them otherwise. It was an even bigger privilege to watch them realize it for themselves. My favorite question to ask the students was always, "What's your favorite part?" They'd point to a line or a stanza and smile proudly at the comparison or the connection they had drawn. They honestly believed they were good, and they were.

These kids wrote valiantly, and they deserve to be praised for it. Hopefully, whether they want to continue writing or not, they will carry with them a little confidence into whatever their future holds, believing that they can be successful at things they never thought they'd be successful in, and keeping with them the honesty that was so humbling to me this summer.

Kendall M., Jr.

Age 6, Saint Florian

Skates

This is the story of my first time skating.

My sister taught me skating.
I love my sister.

Mamaw and Papaw

My mamaw and papaw died. My mother told me. I was sad. I was like five or four. I cried and I missed them. They gave me candy whenever I went to their house. They were round, different colored candies that tasted like peppermint. They always took me to the zoo. I saw spider monkeys and the dolphin show. Sometimes if you're down by the water, you get wet. But you're not in the water! I saw bat. I saw the orangutan.

Cleats

I love my cleats.

I wear them at football.

They help me run fast. We always win! Sometimes I wear them to go to soccer practice too. On Wednesdays we practice and Sundays we play. I kick in practice and I block in the game. I'm the goalie.

House

I am mad. My brother scared me because he was behind me. He snuck up behind me. I didn't know he was there. And when he touch me, I cried. I don't like how he scares me. I turn around STOP.
The END

Morgan W.

Age 10, Saint Florian

When I Got My Tonsils Taken Out: The Original

It was July 27, 2012. The time was 6:00 a.m...I went to St. Vincent's hospital. I was getting my tonsils taken out. I had to wait another hour to sign the paperwork and wait for the doctor. When I went in the room, it was dark green, with a big TV, chairs that were brown, and a bed for me. I waited another hour for the doctor. By then it was eight o'clock in the morning. When the doctor came in I was already wearing my clothes that the nurse gave me. The doctor gave me this thing that smelled like cherries. He said this would put me to sleep. The doctor took me to the special room to get my tonsils out. I went to sleep by the laughing gas. It smelled like cherries. Everything was done by 11 a.m. I had to stay another hour for the doctor to tell me things about the surgery. Then I got sprite, ice cream, and more ice cream. My whole family came to support me. I couldn't talk for six weeks. I was sad because I missed a couple weeks of the third grade. Also I couldn't talk and I love to talk. But I was happy that everything was over after the six weeks. There was great things about it too. I got three years of ice cream.

The Scary Day

Every time I meet up with my family I hear the same story. The story when my mom's front two teeth got knocked out with a baseball bat. It was 1994 and my mom was at a middle school baseball game and she got really good seats by the batter. It was the second morning when tragedy struck. The batter swung back, then *thud*...my mom's teeth were out and bleeding. Here is the bad thing they weren't baby teeth! She started crying and bleeding at the same time. My grandparents rushed my mom to the dentist. So they put in fake teeth and she still has them to this day.

This is the Story about How I Thought my Life was Over...

It was February 21, 2011. It is a really sunny day in Indianapolis. I was getting dressed for my best friend's birthday party. On the way to Chucky Cheese my best friend gets in a really bad, terrible car accident. Then my dad gets a call from her parents telling them to go to Ruth Lily Hospital. I stayed at home with my sister. When my parents came back home they had very bad news. They told me that my best friend died in the car accident.

My friend had short twisted hair. She was turning seven years on that day. She was short and fun sized. She never even got in trouble at home and at school. In school she got straight A's and also when she saw people getting bullied she would stop it at first sight.

Karla G.

Age 14, La Plaza

La Casa de los Sueños

Mi casa es blanca por fuera pero tiene muchos colores por dentro. Colores brillantes y el Suelo de madero. Con 4 Cuartos y 4 baños. y tiene un porche de madera. También tiene el pasto verde y Cortado. Un árbol gigante en frente de su casa pero la hojas colgando. Ese es un árbol diferente a los de mas es mágico y ese árbol representa la paz. Y tiene un columpio en donde yo me encuentro con Dios. Mi casa tiene Ventanas y muchas. Su olor es como el océano. Tiene una reja en las orillas. Y muchas flores de colores que atraen las mariposas. Por las noches estoy viendo netflix con mi familia. Tengo 3 hijas y un esposo que me ayuda a limpiar y a cocinar. We both paid and spoil each other. Todos tenemos comunicación entre nosotros. Mis hijos tienen su propio cuarto. Pues yo ya estoy Graduada de Psicología. Por las noches veo las estrellas y pienso en todo lo que hice y lo que voy a hacer.

The Old House

The old house was dirty, empty and haunted. The walls were falling down. The concrete floor was Cold. The windows were broken and I was living next to the old house. I was 7 years old. She died there. The walls were pale yellow like when she died. Cold in the night hot in the day. Watching a movie in the bedroom with my sister laughing and joking. Her voice was sweet. But the later we heard a woman's laugh because the window was open. I looked but there was nothing. We stop laughing. We turn off the TV. I was scared. I was trying to sleep. My sister close the window. A Drop falling another drop falling. I Close my eyes.

Prove It

When the innocent girl was 9 years old, the poison girl was trying to get her mad, so that everybody would think she is not that innocent. One day the innocent Karla was walking. The poison girl saw her walking. She started to push down her head, because she was sitting in the grass. Karla told her to stop. But She kept on going. The innocent girl asked her to stop 5 more times. She got up and slapped the poison girl. They got into a fight. This beautiful dark skin woman came and stopped them. The poison girl left really mad.

She learned how to self-control and even "Innocent" people get mad too. And that you don't have to prove if someone is bad or good.

I Am...

I am Karla G.
My name means strong, free
I am Tall, creative, cool, funny
I wonder if Aliens exist
I hear a waterfall
I see a big tree with fog
I taste cupcakes
I smell chocolate
I feel water and sand.
I feel weak when I see blood

I knew I was Latino when I spoke Spanish in my house and I ate some Mexican food. A Latino sounds like...My name means *strong* and *free*. I think *free* because sometimes I do what I want. *Strong* because I always forgive and never cry.

Katherine A.

Age 13, La Plaza

I Knew That I was Latina Because…

The day that I heard my mom talk different than she usually does, I started talking like that. My mom thought that it was just her hearing that. So whenever I said, "Chido," she said, "It's just my imagination. It's just my imagination," but in Spanish. I was only 6 and she thought that I was starting to hear people talk like that and I just wanted to talk like that, too. I started saying more Latino words, and when I turned 8 I told her that it was because I was turning more "Latina." She was surprised.

Da – Shadow – Boy

One day in kindergarten me and my mom were in the car and my step-dad (My favorite one) was driving the car to school. There was this song on the radio and it was my mom and my favorite song. The artist that was singing was Natalia Jimenez, a Hispanic artist. When we got to school I didn't want to get out of the truck because of the song my mom said that 5 min more and we both stayed in the car. Every time when I heard the song I remember how much I love music, how much I studied the flute and the piano to get this far, and how much music means to me. Music is my inspiration, my world, and it describes. I feel I calm down because music and "Songwriting" helps me get my feelings out. When I want to make a song is when whenever one of my emotions come out. Like (happy, sad, angry, lazy, or I just feel bored). What I want to get out of the song is nothing really. I just like it as a hobby.

The Birthday Piano

One day I went with my mom Maria to a piano store and me and my mom entered the store and she went to the aisle where the little pianos are and I was where this woman was playing a piano. When she left I got on the piano my mom said that she was looking for me all over. So when the woman left I touch the piano and just stared at it then started playing it. My mom heard me then she followed the noise she saw it was me playing the piano. When I got off she said that I turned around and saw her. She carried me and told me to not do that again and that she was surprised.

So not so long ago my mom and me were talking about my b-day. When she came to the conversation of the piano she ask me, "What you want for your b-day?" I said, "Well I would like a piano!" she said, "Well... let me think... you're going to get it!!!" I was really happy because I haven't seen a piano for a long time.

And Hit One Note

My journey started when I was two. My mom and me were passing through a piano store. My mom told me that when we passed we went inside and she was looking at a little piano. Then I was hearing someone playing it. Then when the person left I just looked at the piano, got closer and closer. When I got to the piano I touched it and hit one note. My mom was looking for me and she said she found me so concentrated on the piano. She said that 5 min. later she said that she was surprised and she carried me and we left. Now, my mom and me were talking yesterday if we could make money to buy a piano. She said, "Of course." She was really wanting to have one since that accident happened.

Rita Mitchell

Student Teacher, La Plaza and Saint Florian

Being a Good Writer

My service with the Indiana Writer's Center, Build A Rainbow program has been an eye opener this summer. This was my first time working with B.A.R. and I am grateful for the experience. The program is one of the most authentic establishments that allow writers to creatively tell their stories without fear of being wrong in some way. Being a good writer is a craft but if smothered, beaten down, or criticized it will not flourish. As long as I have been writing I still get jitters about sharing my thoughts on paper. The amount of tons that weigh on my hand every time I pick up a pencil or type on a computer is heavier than anyone will ever know. These young writers are at an age where honesty and creativity is often purged from their system for false fillers. I could vividly see a line between students of more or less years of schooling. The kids with more schooling seemed to have more apprehension when faced with a blank page. I only mention this to say that above all I admire them. The bravery these young writers have shown in their writing and when sharing has earned my respect and camaraderie. I am honored to have experienced and read so many great works by many who are half my age or less. My greatest moments came from being able to work with them one on one. Those moments meant the most to me because it placed me in the writer's position. The beauty of working through their writing challenges alongside them made the journey to their memoirs all the more precious. Through working with them I have learned more about myself as a person and writer. The advantage of their now published works is that we all have the ability to reminisce and relate to their stories. I thank these writers for their hard work and diligence writing their stories and I thank you the reader for now listening and remembering…

Jordan J.

Age 10, Saint Florian

It's the Best Day Ever

To me it was the best day ever when my nephew and niece was born 'cause my niece is 1 and my nephew is 7 months. So one day he is going to be a Linebacker Someday for the Indianapolis Colts and my niece I going to be his manager. He's going to be a Linebacker 'cause he's already 9 pounds that's amazing 'cause my niece is 10 pounds. My nephew has curly hair and my niece has puffy hair. So if you take her band off it's going to be frizzy and they love to smile and take/snatch food from people like once they were at my house and DJ snatched his bottle from me and Sha took my hamburger and they love toys like basketball and foam footballs. They love scary shows and Sha loves hot stuff like hot fries, hot Cheetos, takis, and hot sauce and she doesn't cry she and my nephew are cool and relaxed. It makes me feel proud that they're in a safe environment and they're going to be famous and she and DJ are going to share money with me even though I'm going to be famous.

Follow Me

Once my brother and me went with my neighbor to the park and were playing basketball and this dude had on a Kobe jersey and kept saying my friend sucks So he dunked on him and my brother big-manned him. I was playing basketball with Rodrick and I kept scoring on him and splashing threes on him I was wearin' my zoom soldier 7s they are red black and white. Then when we were driving home and this lady kept thinking we were following her then she cussed her out and my neighbor said if I had let my dog out she would have got scars and blood all over her face the end.

Melody B.

Age 10, Saint Florian

Florida

Yes! I'm out of the one digits and in the 2-digits—that moment felt so happy I'll never forget it. My mom decided to plan a trip not just for my Birthday but just to get out of the house. So let's say we're already in Florida and me and my sister call out palm trees and then we're at the condo resort and the best part was we're on the beach, so then [April 1] came. It was my b-day. We got to go on a cruise for my b-day for 3 hours. I had fun. We got to eat but for dessert was cheesecake with a candle but I didn't like cheesecake so I blew the candle out and gave it to my brother. It's important for you to know my story because it's amazing, wonderful, and everyone should like (I would hope) Florida and it's great to celebrate b-days.

(hearing) boarding the cruise and the siren going honk honk "Let's go to Florida"
(feeling) inpatient, excited, butterflies flying free, happy
(seeing) paradise right in front of me, palm trees, green grass, people, stores, beach, condo

The Shoes

I remember the time my brother Deonte went to the mall in a blizzard just to get a pair of shoes. So it all started when Deonte ask if he can use my mom's credit card for the 50th time I'm guessing? "No!" "Please!" "NO!" "Please!" "I promise I'll give you the money back!" You can probably tell that's my brother and my mother talking, but this is the part where I come in. "Deonte you always say you're going to give mommy the money back but we both know sometimes you forget." "Was anyone talking to you!" "You're really mean. You know that right." "Mom, tell her to go outside or something." "Mel, go upstairs please and do something. Deonte I with give you the card but If you come back with more than a pair of shoes you're not going to buy anything with my credit card ever again." "OOK," 1 hour later... "Mom Deonte's back ha, look at him in the blizzard holding the pair of shoes he got. Mom you're laughing so hard New Jersey can here you." Deonte came through the door. "At least I got my shoes."

I Remember

The first time I joined NRG dance company
The first time I won one of my dances
I met Brooke my step sister
I met my step dad
When I joined Eagle Elementary School
I went to Holiday World for the first time and more
I got on the Raven at Holiday World
The time I went to Kings Island for my step sisters B-day
The first time I was in my 2-digets—at Florida.

The Stepdad's Slimy Nose!

Swoosh! "Drink it No come on drink it."

I remember the time I tried to get revenge on Mr. Victor but instead of him drinking it my mom drunk it. So I was downstairs with my family and then suddenly I found a pair of binoculars on the dining room table. I grabbed them and ran into the orange room. Everyone was down there. So I decided to put on the binoculars and go around touching the tip of everyone's nose. But then I got to Mr. Victor and I tried to touch the tip of his nose but instead of touching the tip of his nose he jerked his head forward and I missed the tip of his nose and my finger slipped into his slimy disgusting nose I immediately took my finger out and washed it more than once. When I finished washing my finger I went up to him and said that was more disgusting than touching worms!

So I got him back by getting him a cup of water and spitting into the cup. Then I said, "I got you some water" but he said I didn't ask for water. So I said, "If I drink it will you drink it?" He said no but my mom said, "Yes" but I hesitated and said it's for Mr. Victor. So I said ok so I drunk some of it then my mom took a sip of the water with spit then I cracked up. And she asked me, "What did you put into the cup of water?" "I spit a little into the cup." And she was in shock and I said it was for Mr. Victor! Then everyone but my mom and Mr. Victor laughed.

Isreal L.

Age 9, Saint Florian

I am...

I am Isreal
I am red and purple
I am Old Colony Road
I am pizza
I am basketball and Subway Surfers
I am Spider-Man
I am Nikki Minaj
I am Monkey Joe's
I am Yeppee
I am Oh Man

Landed on My Feet

One time I was trying to be cool. SO I jumped off of a swing and I fell. I did it because I wanted my friends to think I'm really cool. So I jumped off the top of the plastic house. I said ouch and still landed on my feet. It was awesome.

Six Pack Laughter

One time I laughed so hard that my stomach turned into a six pack. My friend then made my stomach into a 6 pack. It was so funny. I forgot what Steven said. Then he wanted me to make his stomach turn into a six pack. So I told a Joke but it didn't work. Steven weighs 130 pounds. I said you have to be skinnier. Then Steven fell on me. Then I said, "You're busting all six of my packs." Steven said, "For the last time, you do not have a six pack."

The Ring of Fire

This is the story of what happened when I was riding the Ring of Fire. It was at the carnival. Me and my cousins rode it together. When the ride started it went slow and as it started to go all the way around. It sped up to about 35mph. I was scared and ducked under the seat.

I remember riding the Ring of Fire. It felt very weird. I say that because I hung upside down for a long time. I did not scream. I kept my eyes shut and hung under the belt. I was scared.

Lyrik E.

Age 12, Saint Florian

Laughing Pain

A time when I laughed so hard that I almost peed on myself was when me, Breanna, Amari, Joslan, Ayana, Tamara, Wesley, Reggie and some other people had to do some wall sits and pushups. Well we had to do that because it was some people was being rude to the art people in camp. To be exact it wasn't funny when people was rude to the art people but then we had to do pushups.

It was funny because the pushups were hurting and Tamara was saying some hilarious things. She said, "My booty and my stomach hurt" and then she was acting like she was crying. Then Wesley was crying and his eyes was bloodshot red. Everyone else was in worse pain and he was the only boy that was crying. Also Tamara's arms was shaking so hard that she could barely get up.

Reggie had his knees on the floor and he thought Mr. Rob didn't see them on the floor because he was far back. Me, Amari, Brenn, Ayana, and Josiah was laughing so hard that we could barely do pushups.

The First Time I Meet My New Baby Nephew

The day I meet my 3rd nephew was on Easter, April 20th. It was a beautiful warm cooling day outside. His name was Brayln and he was the first baby to be born in the Eskenazi hospital. That's what made him very special. When I heard he was born I was excited to see him because I love babies.

When I walked into the cold hospital with my mom, I was in a rush. So we got to the waiting room and had to wait for 3 minutes. As soon as the nurse called us to enter into the room, I jumped up and started to fast walk.

My mom, stepdad, and I entered into the room. Brayln's eyes were shut sleep. I didn't want to wake him so handsome. But as soon as I held him in my hands for the very first time my mom took him. I desperately said you can only keep him for 2 minutes and she just looked at me.

After three minutes passed I took him and he had a head full of hair. His ears were dark and I could tell he was going to be just like his daddy. When he was in my hand, his beautiful eyes were staring into mines, I was just smiling. It was just about to be 9:00 and we had to get home, so I gave him to his daddy and gave him a big kiss goodbye.

Malik H.

Age 9, Saint Florian

Scar

I got a scar. I was on my bike. I was speeding. It was a black scar. It was on my leg.

Someone Said the Word

Bryan was laughing and he said everybody was made out of trash and I telled on him. I was mad. Yup, he got in trouble. Someone said shut up. Someone said the word. There was like 2 people who got in trouble.

Cheez-Its and Ants

The first time I ate Cheez-Its. Cheez-Its taste like cheese pizzas. There are pretzels that taste like pizza, too. Cheez-Its almost look like half brown and half orange. It tastes like half pizza and half crust. My aunt buys Cheez-Its from the store. When she buys them, I feel happy. She buys Cheez-Its for me, because I like to snack on them. And I drink Sprite with them. I was eating one and there were a bunch on the floor one time. And then ants started coming. So I tried to kill them with poison and they all died and I had to throw them away and put them in a garbage truck. Then I went back to eat Cheez-Its and play my video games. The ants look like jelly beans.

Kelly S.

Age 12, Saint Florian

Late Night Pranks

So one day at my basketball tournament, we were at a hotel. My teammates said that the first person to go to sleep was gonna get smacked. My friend Ed went to sleep first so we smacked him with a handful of soap. The last person hit him with a pillow. So right before we smacked him we made sure everyone is situated. So on 3 we smacked him. The last person tapped him on his shoulder and hit him in the face with a pillow. We all started laughing and went to sleep.

My Favorite Shoes

Black, grey and red. My favorite shoe is the Jordan cement 3's I was seven when I first got them. I got them before my basketball game. I played in them. I scored 15 points. The place was called ISSA. I was a tall 7 year old. I could dribble the ball well. The court I played on was dusty. The shoes were mid top. They had a lot of traction. The traction helped me start to run one way and stop run another way. I stopped wearing the shoes because I hurt my ankle so I started wearing hightops. How I hurt my ankle by rolling it. I went up for a rebound and fell on somebody foot. And that is my favorite pair of shoes.

Sleepover

One time I had a sleepover and my cousin was over my house. My little brother was asleep on the Lay-Z-Boy chair. He kicked up the footrest and went to sleep, the chair tipped over so me and my cousin said it is the perfect time to scare him. So I grabbed both of his arms and shook him. We also videotaped so we can look at it. Also my mom yelled at me, but I couldn't take her serious because I was still laughing. My Little brother was very mad he hit me, but I still laughed. Then we went to sleep.

Maiya D.

Age 11, Saint Florian

Cedar Point

The toys I got at Cedar Point is a pink monkey. The people who I went with is my mom, dad, brother, sister, Tianna, Baby J, Sister's friend, Jordan, and nephew's cousin. Baby J, Baby J's cousin, Tianna, and I all got our faces painted after that we went to get something to eat and drink. It was pizza and cola. It was delicious. Soon I felt really fool so I fed some of my bread crust to the seagulls. They seemed to have a big fight over who got the last bread crust so then they tore the bread crust in half, got the bread crust, and left.

So after we digested our food we went to go and get on the roller coasters and Tianna and I were very scared to get on the rides so we decide to get on some kitty rides first to calm us down. After that we went to the rides so we just had to wait in the line to go up to the roller coaster. Soon the line was over we got to finally get on the ride.

Jordan T.

Age 8, Saint Florian

I Remember

I remember the time I rode my first rollicoaster. It was when we took over the camp, so we decided to go to holiday world. As soon as we got in there I wanted to go on the raven but boy did it have a really long line! My cousin Sydney and I rode together and my other cousin went alone. When we all got together we shouted that was FUN! It was fun because we got to go fast. On the rollicoaster we went side to side up and down and we almost went upside down. We went so high and dropped down really fast. And we all had an INCREDIBLE TIME.

I remember on 4th of July I went to my cousin's house. First, I said hi to everybody. Then, I went to jump on the trampoline with my cousins. Then they told me that we were doing fireworks! After fireworks we had to go home because my mom was tired.

I remember at daycare and I was standing on a chair thinking I was superman so I decided to jump off the chair and didn't realize that there was a sharp edge on the carpet and I landed my eyelid on the sharp edge and I almost cut the hole thing off that would have been bad. When they took me to the emergency room it took them a day to set three stitches in WOW!

Josiah H.

Age 13, Saint Florian

Treadmill

I remember a time when I fell off a treadmill. I was at my grandparents' house right. And ah I didn't know how to turn the treadmill. We were already standing on it when I slid this thing up and the treadmill popped on at 800. My brother was thrown off first and he hit the wall facing the back of the machine. I fell on the treadmill and skinned my knee. My grandma put a lot of peroxide on it and then put on a band-aid. My brother just laid there until my auntie picked him up after she turned off the machine.

I Don't Even Do Nothing

I draw boxes when I'm bored. *Wham* 3D Triangle Let's Go! What!? I don't know. I'm ah draw a 3D house or Nah. *Wham*! 3D house. *Wham, Wham, Wham*. I want to color this box in.

I'm From

I come from a loud bossy sister Angela. She is annoying, she is one year older but thinks she's all that. She switches body parts she don't have, pops her gum and acts straight hood. She hits me for no reason every day. For example, I tried to sit in the front seat and she hit me in the back of the head. She was mad because I beat her to the front seat and decided to take her anger out on me. Angela yells at my younger brother Jeremiah, because he wanted to play the Wii. After she was talking crazy Jeremiah hit her, and then she picked him up by his arms and threw him on the couch. He rolled off the couch and hit his head on the table. About a week ago she tried to embarrass us outside in front of her friends. She went outside and screamed that "I was a punk!" Me, a punk? I got tired of her talking so I picked her up and slammed her.

Owen S.
Age 15, La Plaza

My Dad

The person that I admire most is my dad. He has worked hard for me and his family. He always puts his family on thought best to help him work harder than he already has. He brings home money for me to have and save it in my bank account. My dad is the main one who puts food on the table for me and my sister to enjoy and have. Sometimes he comes home with cuts on his fingers and every time I see them it reminds me of how hard he works, so I can have a better future and enjoy, live as I do now.

Name

This is the story of what happened when I was named Cati la Catorina that changed my life forever and I will never forget it. It was a hot summer I had just started summer camp/La Plaza. The day was so hot you could feel the sweat dripping from your forehead down to your body.

But anyway back on topic Cali la Catorina is a ladybug not just lady but it's a homosexual lady bug who is teaching you how to cook but in a funny way. Sometimes her or he I don't know what it is talks in a bad way and nasty but the voice just makes me laugh and creeps me out. In the story of Cati la Catorina she had a partner who was a fly but I thought it was funny how they went in cornbread and when they came back he was dead.

Mark Z.

Age 7, Saint Florian

My Best Friend

Dylan Doss is my best friend. Dylan's favorite color is yellow and Me and Dylan's favorite cartoons are *Teenage Mutant Ninja Turtles* & *SpongeBob SquarePants*. Me and Dylan play basketball on the same basketball team. Me and Dylan both have mohawks. I am 7 he is nine. We play AAU Basketball on the Gardens Magic.

Tooth

This is the story of what happened when my dad pulled my tooth out. My tooth was wiggling for 2 months and it was starting to hurt. My dad had to get a napkin and twist it and he got it out. It didn't hurt but it was bleeding. My dad had to put the tooth in the bag to keep it safe.

Laundry

It was a Tuesday night It was my mom, dad, brother, & my sister in the house. And my mom said she needed to do laundry & she told me to do it so I did it. So I went in the basement and my brother scares me and I drop the clothes! I felt nervous & scared my mom was going to be mad. My brother picked up the clothes and helped me put the clothes in washer and we went upstairs to eat dinner. THE END.

Tracy Line

Volunteer, Saint Florian

Connection, Inspiration and Whispers of the Heart

I wasn't sure I wanted to be there. Because the first day had been a little rough. But as I talked it over with God on my way home that day, I'd heard a still small voice inside say, "Go back." And over the years I've learned to listen to the tiny whispers of my heart, because my heart often knows better than I.

So here I was, back in the aged and less-than-shiny inner city elementary school, hoping this day won't be like the previous one. Hoping my enthusiasm to volunteer in a program where I know no one, in a program that's gone on all summer without me because I was late in learning about it, isn't a bad idea.

The room is cold, and a bit dark as the window shades block the outdoor light. I sit in the tiny plastic chair waiting. Waiting for the other volunteers to file in. Waiting for the instructor to tell us what we'll do on this day of writing camp for the kids of St. Florian. Waiting in truth, to prove that whisper wrong.

In a matter of minutes approximately 40 middle schoolers, most of whom are bigger than me, fill the room, piling into their own plastic chairs. I get up from my empty table and find a spot at one with four gangling boys. One is in constant motion, chattering with kids at another table. One has his head down as if he's asleep. The other two remain quiet, simply staring into space. I'm here for a reason; I want to connect, inspire, encourage others to write. But I too remain silent. My awkward shyness takes over; the words won't come.

The instructor quickly commands the attention of the kids. It's apparent they will listen to her. In fact, if I'm reading the room accurately, I believe they respect her, like her even. The positive energy intrigues me. She begins the first exercise; we are to close our eyes, think about a place we have visited and describe it, remember how we felt about it. I look around and see kids across the room writing as fast as they can, describing their memory one sentence at a time. Only the boys at my table aren't writing. They hold their pencils hesitantly; no words are transferred to paper.

I prod them, what about your house, or your room? Have you ever stayed with a grandma or cousin, or spent the night at a friend's house? The boys stare at me impassively; apparently nothing is coming to mind. I join them in their blankness. Together we sink into a comfortable silence, they not writing, me anxious over my inability to engage them.

But then something happens. One of the boys starts writing furiously. It's one of the quiet ones; he's remembering a trip to his uncle's last summer, and writes about the house, the yard, the garden. The chatty one gets an idea from his friend: he suddenly recalls a trip to the fair and the smells of corn and cotton candy. Another boy puts pen to paper, writing about what I do not know. The one I thought was asleep is actually reading a book; I'll take it. My second day is already better than my first. The first day the kids were restless, wild, didn't trust me, the new volunteer. The first day I also was unsure, as if I too were a middle school student.

But today we interact. I ask the boys what age they are, where they attend school, what they like to do. They are nice, polite, willing to talk to me: a middle-aged suburban mother of daughters who can't possibly know anything about their day-to-day life. I enjoy getting to know them. I ask if I may read what they've written. They willingly show me their work. They are proud, and I am...so impressed with their creativity.

Minutes later the instructor invites the students into the Author's Chair. 39 students remain quiet while 1 sits up front and reads her story. The instructor points out the uniqueness of her writing and we all snap our approval. One by one each student shares his writing. I see smiles and satisfaction cross the faces of the students and know I too, am smiling.

I am inspired by the creativity of these children. I am awed with the fierceness and depth of their writing. I am in love with this understanding that through words, simple words written on a sheet of notebook paper, a forty-something suburban woman can connect with a group of inner city fourteen-year-old boys. If, she has the courage to come back after having a rough first day.

That small voice that whispers inside...It's always right.

Collaborative Poems

Concord

"Starry Night" *By Vincent Van Gogh*

The hills look like waves going back to the sea.
The sky swirls like a tsunami.
We feel the rushing wind like cars going by.
The twisting sky looks like goldfish dust.
We hear the bells of the steeple.
The cypress tree squirms like a shock wave.

"Sunflowers" *By Vincent Van Gogh*

Vincent, why are some of the flowers dead?
Did they grow outside your window?
Do you feel like this is your best painting?
How tall were your sunflowers?
What's in the background? Is it a wall?
I can see the reflection of your flowers in the vase.

Vanessa G.

Age 13, La Plaza

I am...

I am Vanessa
My name means Butterflies
I am Funny, Fabulous, outgoing, strong-minded
I wonder about the afterlife
I hear The birds
I see the beach
I taste chocolate
I smell my mom's perfume
I feel my dog's fur

My name is Vanessa my name means butterflies. I don't know why, maybe because I'm hard to predict, just like butterflies you don't know where they are going next. I'm free like butterflies, there's no restriction for me. I'm wild. I'm happy no matter what I never let people see me sad. I make positive feelings. Just like the people feel colors of a butterfly. I travel, I see different things just like butterflies do when they travel.

I Knew I was Latino When

My mom said that she was going to do a small carne asada. When at the end all her friends were there like 25 kids and like 7 pairs. A bunch of kids running around my house. La carne asada con nopales arroz, Frijoles, and more than, and then it wouldn't end that Saturday night it would last the whole weekend.

Water

Water is mysteriously beautiful. Life's motor. To me water is a hobby. Swimming needs to be done in water. I love swimming it feels that I'm floating in heaven because I'm no longer on my feet. I forget about reality. My entire body relaxes. It has a rhythm, one left foot up, right up.

Being a Butterfly: The Meaning of My Name

My name means *butterfly*. My parents got it out of a name book. I guess it was destiny. The future knew that I was going to be like a butterfly, I'm happy I'm that type of person that no matter if it thunders, rains, snows, I'm smiling. I don't like people sad. I see things differently than what other people see things differently, than what other people see things up above the sky. I transmit a good vibe just like the colors of a butterfly. People think that I'm physically delicate just like the wings of a butterfly. But what people don't is that I protect myself emotionally and physically just like the butterfly does when you try to catch her. I'm free and wild. There's no barriers for me. If I think I can do something, I can. Just like the butterflies!

Collaborative Poem

Concord

I am a Street

I am a street in Indianapolis
With a monument and a circle.
I am the smell of gasoline,
The sound of running motors.

I am 16th Street to Speedway,
The smell of tar and sewer.
I am a trashcan for careless people,
A pathway for the cars.

Chorus:
I am a street in Indianapolis
And it's a dream come true
Cause if I can be a street in Indianapolis
I can be the road to you.

I am pogo sticks and bicycles,
A street with no dead ends.
I'm the taco truck, the ice cream truck,
The farmer's market every Wednesday.

I am potholes and patches
Like rough skin where it's dry.
I'm a home for homeless people,
I'm divided with yellow lines.

I am the excitement of a parade
With bright trumpets and tubas.
I'm the song, "The More We Get Together,"
The stop and go of traffic.

Chorus:
I am a street in Indianapolis
And it's a dream come true
Cause if I can be a street in Indianapolis
I can be the road to you.

I am the Chase Tower with horses
And carriages trotting past.
I'm the dead bird on the asphalt,
I am your address.

I am a street in Indianapolis
With a monument and a circle.
At night I'm hard to see
But as bright as the stars.

Chorus:
I am a street in Indianapolis
And it's a dream come true
Cause if I can be a street in Indianapolis
I can be the road to you.

Lyrics by Concord Summer Camp 2014
Chorus and Music by Iona Wagner

Shari Wagner

Lead Instructor, Concord

"I am a Street": Our Collaborative Process

One of my favorite activities with any poetry writing class, whether that class is composed of adults, children, or seniors, is to have it write a collaborative poem. I introduce the topic, read one or two poems that serve as models, and then have members of the class contribute lines orally. Participants can build on a previous image that someone has offered (i.e. extend the line by making it more specific) or they can start a new line. My role is to ask questions that steer the class toward specificity, sensual language, and metaphor. Alliteration and assonance often appear naturally in these spoken lines, and when I hear a really nice example I point it out. Just a bit of extra praise for a striking image or a playful use of sound and rhythm works to engender more of the same. The process of writing a group poem not only helps students learn some basic techniques of poetry writing, but it creates a sense of community and gives beginning poets confidence before starting their own poems on a similar topic.

As I was planning this summer's poetry workshop at Concord Neighborhood Camp, I thought about how much fun it might be if I took advantage of my daughter's songwriting skills and had her set one of our collaborative poems to music. I thought a poem about a place might work especially well for this project, and as I thought about models, Mary Chapin Carpenter's wonderful song "I Am A Town" came to mind. The lyrics, which describe a small town in Carolina, have the sensual detail that I wanted to encourage in my students' poem, and the repetition of the phrase "I am . . ." would be an easy list form for us to use. We read "I Am A Town" aloud in class and then my middle school students took off with lines describing what they know of Indianapolis streets. Charnell Peters, one of our college interns, wrote down the lines on a dry erase board, and they came so quickly we had to take breaks so she could catch up. I loved the group's wide-ranging and vivid descriptions of sounds, smells, sights, and even textures. "I am the feeling of rough skin when it's dry," said one student. Another added, "I am potholes and patches."

I knew we had terrific lyrics, but I also knew that the lines would be much easier for my daughter to work with if they were grouped into stanzas that had some consistency in rhythm. As I played around with the order of the lines, they started to fall easily into quatrains. For the sake of that form, I had to let go of a few of the images, but mostly the language stayed the same—just tightened for rhythm and the order rearranged. Iona, who will be a senior in high school, added a chorus that suddenly took the song to a new dimension, making it a love song: "I am a street in Indianapolis / And it's a dream come true / Cause if I can be a street in Indianapolis / I can be the road to you."

Iona composed the melody for "I am a Street" on the piano, but she transferred it to guitar in order to share a live version with the class. The students and interns and volunteers were all excited to see how our collaborative poem had evolved into a bona vide song. You can read the lyrics to that ballad in this book and hear it sung on YouTube (http://tiny.cc/iamastreet). Writing is often viewed as a solitary process, but our project illustrates how it can also be collaborative.

Nuri R.

Age 16, La Plaza

Star-Gazer

I used to star gaze all the time.
With my fuzzy curls fanned out
Messily on the grass, I would just lay
and stare at the sky. It scarred me in the
most fantastic way. My heart race hand in-
hand with my imagination.
How did the stars become the stars?
How did the sky become THE SKY? I couldn't
Wrap my mind around the concept.
Conflicting theories of scientific background
and religious stories that were spooned
fed to me duked it out
to be the winner in my head. But with my
head resting on the plush pillow of grass, I
slowly drifted to an answer. And I still
slightly believe my idea to this day. In my
ignorant youth, I imagined the stars was
just lights seeping through tiny notes of the
universal wallpaper.

Problems With the World

I believe with every fiber in my being, that we are all born with a certain innocence. With a certain purity and a definite clarity. So for some to tell me that we, as people, are born racist, are born Christian, are born ugly, born gay, born black, born white, yellow, born anything other than human is plain crazy to me. Society instantly labels individuals and places them in pre-set categories.

I was born as crap
I'm seen as crap
I'm treated like crap
But my roots reach all the way
To the tropical islands
To the dark golden skin
To the lushes tress swaying in the wind
And yet they see me as crap
They talk to me like crap
They look at me like crap
But my heritage connects me
all they way back to the mother lands
To the multitudes of African dialects
To the spiritual dances around the fire
To the once rich lands of gold
Yet you avoid me like crap
You isolate me like crap
You hurt me like crap...

Place

I hated it at first. Like come on. It literally was the size of a shoe box, with plain white walls and its lame side window. The window didn't even open up to a decent view. All we could see was brick, brick, and more brick with a sliver of the sky peeking through. Not a chunk, not a slice. No, just a measly sliver of the sometimes blue and sometimes gray sky.

It was either too cold, like the type of cold where you were shivering in your seat all day or extremely hot. And on those hot days, one not so in shape kid in your class would have giant sweat stains down their pits and clear liquid dripping off their faces. Could the dang school not afford a regular thermostat? One that didn't only have two choices: Saharan desert's stove top or Antarctica's refrigerator. And don't even get me started on the desks. I would sit down in my seat, slide my legs under my desk and bang my shin on the desk leg. I swear it almost never failed. That year I really did consider renting myself a wheelchair, because my poor banged-up shins were just too much for me to handle. Yes, I hated my freshmen year first period classroom.

I Hate You...

curls, upon curls
In addition to your flawless face
You are the definition of gorgeous
And...
And I hate you
as you take your beauty in vain
and you hair flip ours out of your presence
I decided I hate you
Bat your dark lashes all you want
And hike your already too short dress higher
I truly don't care
And...
And I truly don't like you
Why are you sacrificing your brain
For a chance to be in the spotlight with your beauty?
That makes you dumb,
That makes all the work of the diligent women
Before you go to waste
And that makes you irrelevant
At least...
At least irrelevant to me, anyway
With your cleavage all in the open for all to see
And your rosered painted nail manicured to perfection
Oh, let's not forget your desired body
Dear lord,
You irritate me beyond explanation
And yet, you are me...

I Am This and I Am That

I am chipped fingernail paint. I've been doused in layer upon layer of teaching and ideas. But slowly I break through the multitudes of life lessons and imposed morals to find a more natural, original version of myself.

I am a towel. Everyone uses me to wipe away their misery and mistakes. I wrap myself around them in support as they drip their pains onto me. But in the end, they forget about me, and I'm hung out to dry.

I am kinky hair. Seen undesirable by most, I'm hidden under a lie. Yet no one know that under that big lie, is the truest and most realest me they could ever imagine.

I am a ponytail holder. I'm always trying to hold together my faith, my family, and my education. I tightly grip the concepts till my knuckles fade to white. Till I'm stretched to the very brink of breakage. And in the end, I eventually have to let a strand of my life slip from my grasp.

I am a blank sheet of paper. I bask in my pureness. Uninked by the outside world. Free from the stains of the tainted ones. But when the world sees I am not one to follow their scribbled ways, they crumple me up and throw me to the side.

I am a rolly polly bug, when I'm scared of the unknown, I shrink into myself. I put a protective layer around me and hide from the giant foot of life that come down to crush me. But when all is quiet and calm, I open up again and sun bathe in the lovely rays of life.

Writing Prompts

Below find the writing prompts for each of the three unique sites served by Building a Rainbow in 2014. We share these prompts in the hope that you too will write and have your voice be heard.

Saint Florian Writing Prompts

Write "I remember..." and the first memory that comes to mind. Keep doing this for 3-5 minutes, repeating "I remember" each time, writing no more than two-three, tops—sentences per memory. Count the number of memories you have. Then choose one that you want to write about, and tell the story of what happened when...

Tell the story about what happened when something or someone made you mad.

Tell the story about what happened when you had to make a hard choice.

Tell the story about what happened when something made you laugh so hard your belly hurt—or worse!

Tell the story about what happened when you lost someone or something special to you.

Tell the story about what happened when you did something for the first time.

Tell the story about what happened when you had the best day ever.

Tell the story about what happened when you ate your favorite food.

Tell the story about what happened when you wore your favorite pair of shoes.

Draw a map of your neighborhood. Draw an "X" where something happened that you will always remember. Tell the story what happened there.

Tell a story that your family loves to tell about you or another family member.

Do you have a scar? Tell how you got it.

Tell the story about what happened when someone did something that really helped you.

Tell the story about what happened when someone played a trick on your or embarrassed you in some way or you played a trick on someone.

Tell the story about what happened when you did something and then felt sorry about it later.

La Plaza Writing Prompts

Write: If you could have any superpower, what would it be and why?

Write about a place that is important to you.

Write about technology that is important to you, then try 12 hours using no technology (nothing that boots up) and write about your experience.

Write about a food that you love and that's important to your family.

Write: "I am…" a choice of how you define yourself and what influences how you're defined. Prompt #2 (follow up): I know I am Latino because…

Your hero's journey: Write about a quest you undertook—a series of steps toward doing something important that required your overcoming obstacles.

Archetypes: What are the most important roles you play in life or the most important aspects of your personality? Write about that.

Write about something you're good at doing.

Your life as a fairy tale: Write a story from your life that has a moral—that taught you a lesson, a "once upon a time" story. Then write that story as a fairy tale, casting each person and significant thing involved as a character or object common to classic fairy tales.

We have objects, possessions, items in our lives that have great symbolic value. Write and describe anywhere from one to five objects that have value to you, explain why they are significant, and then think of them symbolically. What do they represent besides just themselves or their dollar value?

Concord Writing Prompts

Poem about a Family Member: Write a poem about a person in your family who means a lot to you. This might be a grandparent, a parent, a sister or brother, an aunt or uncle . . . or someone who is not actually a family member but seems like a family member to you.

Poem about a Family Outing: Write a poem about a family outing that was important to you. You might write about a vacation to a certain place or a trip to see relatives. You could write about one or more visits to your family's favorite restaurant or park. You might write about a wonderful outing or one in which everything went wrong.

A Poem Describing an Object: Write a poem about the object you find in your grab bag. Use details, comparisons, metaphors, and sensory details.

A Poem about a Teacher: Write a poem that describes or tells a story about a favorite teacher (a school teacher, a camp counselor, a coach, a parent, etc.) or about a time when you were a teacher, when you taught someone else to do something, like how to ride a bike or how to count.

A Poem about a Favorite Place: Write a poem about a place you feel connected to in a special way. This might be the kitchen in your house, a location in your yard or along your street, a classroom in your school, or somewhere you go with friends or a grandparent. This should be a place you enjoy returning to, if only through memory or imagination.

Poem Inspired by the Nina Mason Pulliam Ecolab, Marian University: Write a poem describing your walk through the Marian University Ecolab. You can describe the whole walk or just focus on one or more plants or animals that you find interesting. You can include yourself in this poem and also other people. You might include something our guide says. Use comparisons and details that paint a picture and appeal to the senses. Surprise your readers by thinking outside of the box!

Poem Inspired by a Van Gogh Painting: Write a poem inspired by your print of a Vincent Van Gogh Painting. Before you start to write your poem, you may want to make a list of things you see in the painting and things your imagination can almost hear, smell, taste, or touch. Possible strategies:

—Speak directly to the person in the painting.

—Speak directly to Van Gogh about his painting.

—Use the painting as a starting point and then imagine a story that continues. Or imagine a story that came before what you see in the painting.

Poem Creating a Self-Portrait: Write a poem that tells the reader how you would like to be drawn (or painted) or how you would like to be portrayed in a sculpture or monument. Your poem should reveal who you are: for example, what you like or don't like about yourself, what you want people to know about you and remember, what you think is important in life or what you feel like inside.

Andrea Boucher

Cover Artist Statement

If you ever want your spirit refreshed, your altruism sparked, and your heart inspired, go sit in on a writing session for the Build a Rainbow program.

I started the MFA Creative Writing program at Butler University last fall. Through my work there with Pressgang (a small publishing press affiliated with Butler), I connected with Barb Shoup and Lyn Jones of the Indiana Writers Center, and they asked me to do the cover design for this year's anthology. To give me a feel for what Building a Rainbow is all about, I was invited to attend some of the writing sessions so that I could observe and interact with all of our young Indianapolis writers.

As I drove to my first session visit, I didn't know what to expect and was even a little nervous. I hadn't been around a group of kids in a very long time. What would they be like? I imagined different scenarios ranging from embarrassing to neutral. What I didn't imagine was the best case scenario, where I would leave these sessions with a buoyancy in my step that would last for days. You can't be in the presence of so much energy and enthusiasm and not become soaked in it yourself. As you get older, you may realize that you have inadvertently created a box around yourself based on habits and routine. This box exists in your writerly world as well. Listening to these kids come up with fresh ideas, unlimited by the rules and rote of grown-up life, was eye-opening for me and took down a side of my invisible box that I hadn't even known was there. Using the same writing prompts the teachers had given the children, I went home after each session and did my own writing. But something was different. I was able to write with an unencumbered zest, the disapproving censor in my mind shushed. Go ahead and use silly words, make unusual comparisons — write just for the joy of it! And be proud of your effort: *you are writing*. Thank you to all of the kids at Concord, La Plaza, and Saint Florian for reminding me of this fact. I hope you like the cover. You are incredible!

I also want to commend all of the people who run this program and teach the kids. Many qualifiers come to mind: organized, prompt, thorough, invested, passionate, devoted, tireless, reverent. They all care so much. They treat these young writers with respect. Whether the writer was seven years old or fifteen didn't matter; all writers were equal and commended for the very fact that they were creating. You could see in the children's smiles how good they felt to be validated and watch as their self-regard lifted, which in turn created joy in the teacher. It was a beautiful symbiosis, as marvelous as a rainbow. I am so happy to have been a part of it.

Artist Biography

Andrea Boucher is currently earning her MFA in the Butler University Creative Writing program. After building a career in the corporate world as an editor and technical writer for various companies, she decided to do what she really wanted in life, which is to be a literary nonfiction writer who moonlights as a book designer. In addition to this anthology, she also designed and typeset the anthology for the Central and Southern Indiana *2014 Scholastic Art & Writing Awards*.

Acknowledgements

The Indiana Writers Center gratefully acknowledges the support of these organizations and individuals:

Executive Director:
Barbara Shoup

Education Outreach Director:
Darolyn "Lyn" Jones

Instructors:
Darolyn "Lyn" Jones
Kip Robisch
Barbara Shoup
Shari Wagner

Teaching Assistants:
Michael Baumann
Corrie Herron
Malia Sandberg

Interns:
Taylor Frymier
Olivia Gehrich
Rachel Johnson
Rita Mitchell
Charnell Peters

Volunteers:
Paige Bolen
Patricia Cupp
Carole Evans
Barbara George
Jennifer Hawke
Brad King
Will Lagunas
Tracy Line
Mary Redman

Editing Team:
Mark Latta
Darolyn "Lyn" Jones
Michael Baumann
Olivia Gehrich
Rachel Johnson
Charnell Peters

Organizations:
Arts Council of Indianapolis
Allen Whitehill Clowes Charitable Foundation, Inc.
Concord Neighborhood Center
Indiana Arts Council
Indianapolis Foundation
La Plaza
Lilly Endowment
Marian University Writing Center
Saint Florian Center
Summer Youth Program Fund
Wallack, Somers & Haas

Index

Chauncey A. 26
Joseph A. 178
Katherine A. 198
Marcel A. 134
Dylan B. 146
Melody B. 202
Randy B. 168
Skylar B. 138
Sydney B. 100
Michael Baumann 108
Ashantē C. 36
Fredy C. 101
Jeffrey C., Jr. 90
Joshua C. 176
Lauren C. 171
Quanell C. 120
Tianna C. 154
Trinity C. 112
Tylen C. 148
Patricia Cupp 126
Caden D. 70
Caleb D. 46
Dominique D. 144
Jacob D. 16
Kenzik D. 98
Maiya D. 210
Nia D. 158
Roman D. 118
Tyree D., Jr. 162
Jeremiah E. 76
Lyrik E. 206
Jesus F. 68
Taylor Frymier 37
Alena G. 9
Amiia G. 14
Da'Laysia G. 121
Danny G. 24
Javier G., Jr. 95
Jeffrey G. 34
Karla G. 196
Wesley G. 110
Vanessa G. 218
Victor G. 163
Olivia Gehrich 50
Alyssa H. 28
Chelsey H. 82
Eduardo H. 44
Elijah H. 152
Enas H. 66
Jeremiah H. 74
Josiah H. 212
Lauren H. 182
Malik H. 208
Nakaih H. 184
Corrie Herron 60
Trevon I. 159
Allen J., Jr. 2
Aylin J. 12

Bayleigh J. 22
Jaime J. 136
Jaquayla J. 124
Jordan J. 201
Rachel Johnson 91
Lyn Jones 29
Jalen K. 130
Jeremiah K. 86
Anyiah L. 48
Hope L. 186
Isreal L. 204
Joniece L. 188
Luis L. 178
Malaki L. 142
Morgan L. 114
Tracy Line 215
Andrew M. 1
Bogart M. 18
Chris M. 27
Elyjah M. 58
Jackeline M. 102
Kendall M., Jr. 193
Stephanie M. 32
Sterling M., Jr. 104
Will M. 149
Rita Mitchell 200
Breanna N. 80
Dylan N. 6
Savannah N. 163
Serenity N. 126
Counselor Nichole 69
Counselor Niki 127
Alexis P. 10
Armundo P. 72
Ayana P. 33
Camran P. 20
Javier P. 61
Kailey P. 189
Charnell Peters 190
Desmond R. 62
Hugo R. 106
Ivan R. 54
Jocelyn R. 166
Marlene R. 174
Nuri R. 224
William R. II 131
Mary Redman 116
Ahlena S. 7
Amari S. 84
Angeles S. 78
Austin S. 88
Azhure S. 4
Chase S. 75
Dana S. 56
Kelly S. 209
Owen S. 213
Rafael S. 128
Malia Sandberg 79
Anton T. 53
Jasmine T. 122
Jordan T. 211
Lenabel T. 180
Marquia T. 172
Counselor Mya T. 65
Reggie T. 160
Tamara V. 150
Aasha W. 42
Anthony W. 94
Ashley W. 40
Morgan W. 194
Roderick W. II 156
Sevan W. 140
Shari Wagner..................................222
Mark Z. 214

www.ingramcontent.com/pod-product-compliance
Lightning Source LLC
LaVergne TN
LVHW061248060426
835508LV00018B/1541

* 9 7 8 0 9 8 4 9 5 0 1 4 0 *